The Mysteries of God in a Crisis

By

Julius Chinamo

Printed By

Manufacture and Publishing:

BoD-Books on Demand, Norderstedt

ISBN: 978-3-7526-9086-6

The Mysteries of God in a Crisis

Julius Chinamo

Moorhofsweg 29

OT Spaden

27619 Schiffdorf

Germany

Mobile: +49 176 6917 4950

Email: jchinamo@gmail.com

ISBN: 9783752690866

Contents

The Mysteries of God in a Crisis

Foreword

Going through the various stages of life is like walking through a maze, with many twists and turns. You can stand three feet from the next corner and yet not know what lies behind it. The next step, the next turn will be so close but still

there is mystery behind it. The Christian journey is a mystery, one that alone might not be comprehended. I love the fact that my husband has given us access, the liberty one seldom gives, to walk through the maze that is his life, from birth till now as he has turned the golden age; 40. With every page and every chapter comes an encounter, a lesson, an experience that untangles the mysteries; knot by knot, one after the other.

I know, this Christian journey is not an easy one, but with the information, based on his background, as I mentioned before, is an opportunity for you to lay your story, side by side with Pastor Julius Chinamo's, compare, take notes, learn, take principles, and apply them in your life. What he went through will provide a guideline for your own walk with Christ. What took him two years to figure out will take you the few hours that you will dedicate to reading this book. As we are waiting on God for an answer to our prayers or if we are facing uncertainty know that we have a powerful tool which is the word of God. To us has been availed a rare opportunity to use reality, to apply in our own reality and in no time, you will see the greatness of God in different ways. Ways that will provide you the leverage to rise, to rise so high in your journey with Jesus Christ that your head will be hidden in the clouds. Oh what a blessing!

Cecilia Chinamo

Chapter One.

I want to thank our heavenly Father, our God for giving me this opportunity to speak to many people through this book. I believe someone will be helped after reading this book and change the way they see the greatness of God in different ways. I am personally one of the greatest miracles on this earth, I have heard many stories from my mother about how she miraculously gave birth to me and that how I survived was a big shock to her and the doctors who attended to her during my birth. Now, with such in mind dawns the realization that there are many mysteries of God in the crises in our lives.

As I write this book I am so grateful to God because He has seen me through each and every challenge in my life. I have survived many sicknesses from birth; I also survived a near death accident when I was still at school. It was only the hand of God that fought for me and gave me victory. Glory to Jesus my Saviour! I am now 40years old and I thank God for this milestone. Someone might be surprised as to why I am thanking God for this but I know where I am coming from. My mother gave birth to me and six other siblings of mine, I am number six and all the five who were older than me are now deceased/late. The most painful part is that all of my late brothers and sisters died before they reached 40years of age. I am sure you now have an inclination as to why I am thanking God about this 40th birthday. In life we see God differently and miracles come to people's lives differently as well. Someone who is 80yrs old might not see why I would thank God for being just half of that age, but to me it is a big milestone.

Many times in life we find ourselves in some difficult situations where we are left wondering how God managed to rescue us out of those situations, wondering how we managed to come out. I have discovered that whenever there is a crisis in life is when we see the powerful hand of God. Sometimes we think that God is unaware of whatever situations we might be facing or passing through but alas in His silence is where He is working on our behalf performing miracles. Many times we feel like things are falling apart when they are actually falling into place. People think that their bad situations have nothing to do with God but I am sure after reading this book many will change their views on that.

Before I go much further let me start by defining who God is and what a mystery and a crisis are so that it can help someone to fully understand this book.

A mystery is a religious belief based on a divine revelation, especially one regarded as beyond human understanding or it can be defined as something that is a secret, something where there is no clear explanation, difficult to understand or explain or something unexplainable or unsolvable.

A crisis is a time of intense difficulty or danger, or a time when a difficult or important decision must be made to save a situation, or a turning point of a disease when an important change takes place indicating either recovery or death.

Finally, we cannot proceed without trying to literally define who God is in our lives. In monotheistic belief God is conceived of as the Supreme Being, creator deity, and principal object of faith. God is omnipotent (all-knowing), omnipresent (all-present) and omnibenevolent (all-good) as well as having an eternal and necessary existence.

There are situations in the word of God or in our lives where mysteries or miracles have happened and left many people puzzled. Such occurrences even lead other people who were unbelievers to start believing in Jesus and His wonders. When a mystery is taking place no one has the power to stop it and it just happens suddenly, and leaves many in awe. Whenever something happens that leads to a crisis or a problem the moment God steps in and solves the problem, He does so in a way the human mind cannot comprehend and that is what we call wonders or mysteries of God.

The birth of Isaac

Genesis 21:1-21 New International Version (NIV)

Now the LORD was gracious to Sarah as He had said, and the LORD did for Sarah what He had promised. Sarah became pregnant and bore a son to Abraham in his old age, at the very time God had promised him. Abraham gave the name Isaac to the son Sarah bore him. When his son Isaac was eight days old, Abraham circumcised him, as God commanded him. Abraham was a hundred years old when his son Isaac was born to him.

When God makes a promise to someone He will surely see to it that it is fulfilled even if it takes years. Destiny delayed is not destiny denied, no one has the power to deny what God has promised in someone's life. What can be a long time to men is nothing to worry about in the eyes of God. God fulfills His promises and He does it the moment when everyone is not even expecting it.

Sarah said, *"God has brought me laughter, and everyone who hears about this will laugh with me."* in her mind Sarah could not imagine that she could bear a son in her old age, I always tell people that she probably imagined what people would say about her conceiving at such an old age. God is not moved by someone's age for Him to perform a miracle, He is God. God is not a respecter of man and He does not work the way our science and scientists do. He is beyond biology and physics, under normal circumstances a woman of Sarah's age was past child bearing age, she was even supposed to be in menopause, and it is impossible for someone at that stage to conceive.

And she added, *"Who would have said to Abraham that Sarah would nurse children? Yet I have borne him a son in his old age."* in many situations we write people off or we write ourselves off thinking that God can no longer do a miracle in our lives or in someone's else's life, and in such situations is when God's greatest hand is seen. Never ever write off the greatness of God in one's life, God will never be limited to perform miracles because of age or any situations. I believe there were people who were friends or neighbors of Sarah and Abraham that could never ever believe or imagine them having a child especially considering their advanced age. Never look at your age today and think that it is impossible for God to give you the desires of your heart. God is not concerned with age when He wants to bless someone; a miracle comes where our human mind does not see it fit.

Abraham and Sarah were childless and they were very old and past the child bearing stage. On the other hand, God had promised Abraham that he will be the father of many nations, this sounded hilarious because there was the difficult situation of bareness in Abrahams home. I am sure even Abraham would ask himself as a human being why the Lord would promise him children as many as the sand of the sea or stars of the sky and yet his wife could not give him even a single child. According to medical laws when a woman is no longer menstruating means there is no way she can conceive and also most older people are not sexually active that is probably why Sarah laughed in Genesis 18:12 *So Sarah laughed to herself as she thought, "After I am worn out and my lord is old, will I now have this pleasure?,* this is when the three men believed to be angels prophesied that she will hold a son at the same time the following year, I believe she was imagining the sexual experiences that were to come from that time going forth.

Now in Genesis 21 the whole mystery is seen, I am sure the moment people began to notice that Sarah was pregnant at 80 years old they talked about it because that was something they have never seen before. The whole community might have been shocked, I can see other women wanted to ask her how it happened in her old age, others might have wanted to ask her how it feels being pregnant with the experience and all the changes that pregnancy comes with. Before people could get over the miracle of her pregnancy they saw her now holding a bouncing baby boy named Isaac. What had never been seen in the history of mankind was seen for the first time in the region where they were living. This is how God sometimes works He waits for us to come to the end of our thinking capacity then He starts from there, where we end is where He starts from. This is what I call the mysteries of God in a crisis, in this case it was a crisis of barrenness and at the same time Abraham and Sarah were looking forward to the fulfillment of the promise God had given them, which means whatever God says will surely come to pass no matter what.

Matthew 1:18-25: New International Version

Joseph Accepts Jesus as His Son

18 This is how the birth of Jesus the Messiah came about His mother Mary was pledged to be married to Joseph, but before they came together, she was found to be pregnant through the Holy Spirit. 19 Because Joseph her husband was faithful to the law, and yet did not want to expose her to public disgrace, he had in mind to divorce her quietly. 20 But after he had considered this, an angel of the Lord appeared to him in a dream and said, "Joseph son of David, do not be afraid to take Mary home as your wife, because what is conceived in her is from the Holy Spirit. 21 She will give birth to a son, and you are to give him the name Jesus, because he will save his people from their sins." 22 All this took place to fulfill what the Lord had said through the prophet: 23 "The virgin will conceive and give birth to a son, and they will

call him Immanuel" (which means "God with us").24
When Joseph woke up, he did what the angel of the Lord
had commanded him and took Mary home as his wife.
25 But he did not consummate their marriage until she
gave birth to a son. And he gave him the name Jesus.

Let us also look at what also happened with Mary a young
virgin waiting to be married to Joseph the carpenter, how
she miraculously became pregnant by the Holy Spirit
without physical sex, is something beyond human
comprehension. I can tell whoever is reading this book
that there is no biology or science explanation on how a
virgin becomes pregnant without having sex, worse off,
by the Holy Spirit or how can an old woman who has
passed her monthly periods stage conceive. Surely it can
only be God's ways which are not our ways, how we think
is not how God thinks. Only a miracle from God through
His mysterious ways can make all this possible, He is God
of the impossible. I am really sure even Mary could not
understand what was happening and how this came to pass
in her life, no man could ever understand that mystery that
is why even Joseph was silently thinking of divorcing

Mary because I believe he was failing to comprehend the miracle. Because God was in all of this we see that the moment Joseph wanted to run away from Mary God mysteriously or miraculously visited him in a dream and told him not to do what he was planning for the pregnancy was from the Holy Spirit, the mysteries of God in a crisis. God had to come in His personal being to assure Joseph that his wife did not see another man. God is so amazing brothers and sisters.

1 Chronicles 29 v 11 Yours, O Lord, is the greatness and the power and the glory and the victory and the majesty, indeed everything that is in the heavens and the earth; Yours is the dominion, O Lord, and You exalt Yourself as head over all.

I believe as one is reading this book there is going to be a major understanding of how God works in your life. God is not afraid of situations or any crisis in our lives; He is much bigger than any crisis. And the main purpose in this book is to give the reader more understanding of how God performs His miracles. A crisis does not come to humiliate you; neither does a crisis come in our lives to humiliate our God, never! Every crisis comes to give God a big stage to show who He is in every situation. God is not limited to function because of bad situations but He wants a massive platform where He deals with big problems so that He shines. What you might be calling a problem today might be a stepping stone for God to be seen in your life, that which you are calling a crisis might be exactly the thing which will reveal the greatness of God to many generations to come. When you are facing a problem today rest assured, God will rise to the occasion to reveal his greatness. That sickness inflicting you today, giving you sleepless nights, going to every doctor or a servant of God for prayers just know that it is there for the mighty and powerful hand of God to be seen in that situation. Continue to trust in God He is faithful.

As we continue in unpacking the mysteries of God in our life's crisis we need to focus our minds and pay close attention to our day to day life to notice that some of the things we take lightly or for granted might have been a profound miracle to someone who is not as privileged to have what others have. That pair of shoes you are complaining about, today that you feel is not enough good for you might have been a big miracle to someone who was walking barefoot. That old car that you might be complaining about or the house you are ashamed of can be a big testimony in someone else's life, someone who is praying for a miracle to have a car or place to lay their head. Remember what might be a crisis to someone today might not be a crisis to some so the way people see the hand of God in a situation or crisis might be different depending on the point of view or point of belief. So as you are reading this book do not judge what other people might be seeing as a testimony in their way of life because that might be a normal day to day life to certain communities where there might be nothing to testify about.

Destiny may be delayed but it can never be denied. Do not be moved by a prophecy that has not yet been fulfilled or by something you have been hoping and praying for, for many years and you have not accomplished, never think you have failed. Keep working and praying harder and even if you are delayed it does not mean you are denied.

Psalm 27 v 13 –14. I believe that I shall look upon the goodness of the Lord in the land of the living! Wait for the Lord; be strong, and let your heart take courage; wait for the Lord!

Someone might have wanted to be married and have children at a young age but because of unforeseen circumstances you find yourself still unmarried when you are 40years old, do not worry or despair your time will surely come as long as God is in it. I had tried several times to buy my first car at the young age of 27, but I kept on having many challenges prior to all the plans I had made. But with the God's grace I managed to buy my first car at the age of 36 and it was not an ordinary car, it was a Mercedes. Remember, we might be delayed to our destiny in life but we are surely not denied. Everyone's destiny lies in the hands and plans of God almighty not human beings.

When God wants to show you something new about Himself, or wants you to draw closer to Him and know Him at a deeper level. When God desires to manifest His glory in ways yet unseen by you or He wants to become more real to you, at a level you've never had with Him before. All these things will take place when God allows a crisis in your life.

A crisis is not just a crisis it is never just a crisis. A crisis is always more than a crisis. It is an opportunity to experience and know God to a degree and depth that you have never known before.

Many will read this and think that they are fine right where they are, after all why go through a crisis. No one looks for a crisis or thinks of when their next crisis is coming. Rather, the opposite of that is true, many of us look for a way *out* of a crisis we run from crises and yet a crisis is a prime opportunity for all of us to experience and know God intimately, personally, and profoundly.

When God wanted to reveal Himself at another level to someone in Scripture, it nearly always followed a consistent pattern of crisis. He either allowed, or created, a crisis. During these times, people would find themselves in situations which they themselves could not fix. They came upon scenarios and predicaments that they could not unravel on their own. They ran into unavoidable circumstances. They were in a crisis.

You know you are in a crisis when all of your options are gone. When everything you thought *could* work, doesn't work, when you cannot negotiate your way out of it. You cannot pay your way out of it or talk your way out. When all that you have learned and all that you have tried is not enough to ease the situation you are in, you know you are in a God-ordained, or God-allowed crisis with a purpose.

Chapter Two

In Genesis 37 we read about Joseph, his coat of many colours and about how his brothers sold him onto slavery. When Joseph's brothers became jealous of him because of the love he received from his father Jacob and also because of his dreams, they thought of killing him. One of them then decided that it was better to sell him to the Ishmaelite's as a slave. One thing they did not know was that they were taking him to his destiny, you know my brothers and sisters, when God has ordained you to be someone to go somewhere in life no matter what challenges you might be facing along the way, nothing will stop you from that destiny. What God ordains no one has the power to change or stop. Joseph's brothers interpreted his dreams well but they failed to understand their meaning, which shows us that interpretation of dreams alone without understanding their meaning makes no sense, God can give us a sign but we can fail to see it or interpret the message. In other words, God knew that if these evil brothers of Joseph had known that by selling him they are thrusting him into the right track of his destiny, they would have killed him in order to kill his destiny. If Joseph had remained in the land his father and brothers were living in he would have never seen his destiny. God sometimes uses people you love to take you to your destiny or even those people who hate you can be the ones to take you to your destiny, God can use anyone to take you to your promised land. The brothers thought they are doing evil to Joseph and yet their jealous hearts took him to a place of kingship, Our God works miraculously He is a mystery in Himself.

I do not think that for one minute Josephs brothers ever thought that one day the same dreams they interpreted would be fulfilled. God allowed a crisis in Canaan for the fulfillment of the dream that Joseph had. In other words, God had seen all this before it happened. Usually when people do bad things to someone they are quick to forget but they do not know that what God has ordained does not die a premature death.

I declare to someone today in Jesus' mighty name that refuse to see your destiny die a premature death! Refuse to allow it to be buried alive by the people surrounding you. Because of their evil hearts they forgot Joseph quickly, to them I am sure he was history they thought he was dead and forgotten, but our God does not forget. Even when Joseph asked his brothers about the state of affairs at home and how their father was, they were so hungry all they wanted was food for them and their families back home, they failed to question how or why he seemed to have information about their family, sometimes in life we find ourselves in a crisis that we do not understand and yet it is God who would have allowed such in our lives just to humble us and show His greatness.

Genesis 37 New International Version (NIV)

Joseph's Dreams

Jacob lived in the land where his father had stayed, the land of Canaan.

2 This is the account of Jacob's family line. Joseph, a young man of seventeen, was tending the flocks with his brothers, the sons of Bilhah and the sons of Zilpah, his father's wives, and he brought their father a bad report about them.

I believe the greatest mystery about the life of Joseph was the fact that he was someone very different from the other children of Jacob. The fact that he would bring bad report to his father about his brother's behavior might have meant that was the catalyst that triggered the hatred of his brothers towards him. Sometimes in life we choose to please people and by doing so we divert from the will and plan of God for our lives. It was easy for Joseph to follow suit in the things his brothers were doing but he remained principled because he wanted to reach his destiny. God knew that He had plans for Joseph's life and it was in His plans to fulfill them. Most people miss their destiny because of following the crowd and imitating the bad things that those who we look up to are doing. Joseph could have easily copied and followed what his brothers were doing which was against what their father was anticipating. But, he chose to be different and did things the proper way; he was a principled, Godly young man. It is better to do things alone as long as they are good than to be in a group which does things in a bad way.

3 Now Israel loved Joseph more than any of his other sons, because he had been born to him in his old age; and he made an ornate robe for him.

Another miracle here is that of Jacob having born Joseph in his old age. Brethren God is not moved by what people say or think about someone, when He wants to perform a miracle He does it without consulting anyone. Joseph's character allowed him to be loved by his father more than the other brothers. When you have good character it is automatic that your parents should be happy and proud of you, in the same way, God is proud of those people who live godly lives and He rewards them accordingly. Be a God pleaser not a man pleaser.

4 When his brothers saw that their father loved him more than any of them, they hated him and could not speak a kind word to him.

People with small minds are not able to see or correct areas in their lives where they are wrong but instead they despise people who have a good character. Joseph's brothers should have emulated the good things their younger brother was doing to attract the love of their father. We have encountered people who just hate other people for nothing just because they are good. Do not allow yourself to hate someone who is in right standing with his God because you might end up fighting with God Himself. Do not be moved my dear brethren by what bad people who hate you speak about you as long you are in right standing with God you will still be successful and make it. Let the people hate you but just keep doing the right things, and God will bless you and see His vision for you fulfilled in the mighty name of Jesus.

5 Joseph had a dream, and when he told it to his brothers, they hated him all the more. 6 He said to them, "Listen to this dream I had: 7 We were binding sheaves of grain out in the field when suddenly my sheaf rose and stood upright, while your sheaves gathered around mine and bowed down to it."

When you receive dreams and visions from God, not everything is public consumption because you do not know how that can make the recipients of that dream react. Joseph had no idea of how the brothers would react, not all news is good news in other people's eyes and ears. The dream was so clear that it did not even need a dream interpreter; everyone was so clear as to what Josephs dream meant. Some information needs to be kept as a secret in order to not disturb the smooth flowing of the Spirit of God to give you a testimony. Even when you receive a prophetic word from a servant of God I suggest that you keep it a secret as you wait upon the Lord for fulfillment of the prophecy.

8 His brothers said to him, "Do you intend to reign over us? Will you actually rule us?" And they hated him all the more because of his dream and what he had said.

Look how the enemies of our lives can speak when God is doing something big in our lives. The brothers of Joseph knew that the dream meant that they will be under his leadership at a certain time in life. They did not know that what God has ordained no one will break, the time had come and they were eventually ruled by Joseph. Let people hate you but that does not remove the grace of God and His anointing upon your life. Because Joseph was a good person he did not fight what his brothers were saying and doing against him. Sometimes you block God from doing great things in your life because of either talking too much or wanting to fight your enemies. Let your enemies fight you and do not fight back God will fight the battle for you.

9 Then he had another dream, and he told it to his brothers. "Listen," he said, "I had another dream, and this time the sun and moon and eleven stars were bowing down to me."

I believe at this point Joseph was now aware of his brother's hatred towards him but he just wanted to keep showing them that even though they hated him it did not stop God from giving him dreams that have a clear meaning. Or maybe he would tell them in order to hear their own interpretation of his dreams. Joseph might also have had this attitude of telling his brothers his dreams because he wanted to warn them that what they were doing to him was bad, they were supposed to change and make peace with him since they could interpret his dreams well. In other words, these brothers had a choice of changing their attitude towards Joseph but instead they hated him more.

10 When he told his father as well as his brothers, his father rebuked him and said, "What is this dream you had? Will your mother and I and your brothers actually come and bow down to the ground before you?" 11 His brothers were jealous of him, but his father kept the matter in mind.

When Jacob rebuked his son Joseph concerning this dream he was not disputing the dream's authenticity but I am sure he was now protecting his beloved son hence he kept all these things in his mind. Sometimes our enemies see our progress and destiny before we have even noticed that we are going somewhere, we know this to be true even of demons. I always say to people the one who has possession of the ball is the one who attracts the most attention in the stadium, Joseph was attracting enemies in the form of his brothers because they had seen that he is destined for greatness.

The battle between Joseph and his brothers began because of the dreams he was having. Note that Joseph was not very rich but his dreams were a threat to his brothers. The enemy does not attack you because of who you are today but he attacks you because of who you will be tomorrow. Your future is the reason why you are always under attack; the devil wants you to give up on your future but continue to tell yourself that you will not give up until your dreams come true.

Sometimes we think people are being evil towards us and yet it turned out to be the hand of God to take us to our destiny, your enemies can be used to bless you. I believe Joseph's brothers did the same, they must have felt good after they had sold him to the Midianites but little did they know that they were propelling him to his destiny, to the fulfillment of the dreams which they themselves interpreted so well. I believe we need people like that in life that can be used unknowingly by God to propel us to our destiny although inside them they are thinking otherwise. Joseph was sold to his destiny by his brothers; some people do bad to others not knowing that they are actually fast tracking the destiny of that person. I am not phased when I see people gathered, talking or discussing bad things about me, it makes me want to work even harder to reach bigger and greater levels where they will not be able to reach or see me again. If Joseph's brothers did not develop hatred towards him, I am sure we would not be talking about this now.

After Joseph was sold to the Ishmaelites, he found himself again being sold in Potiphar's house where he was made a slave, then the wife of Potiphar was used to make the dream come true in his life. When you are destined for great heights in life you have to also be prepared to bear the sufferings and challenges which come along the way. Good character is also a big key and a secret to success. Imagine if Joseph had allowed himself to sleep with his boss's beautiful and lustful wife, that was definitely going to be the end of his future and dreams. When you want to go far in life do not allow silly things to divert your focus, great, prominent leaders are the ones who are focused throughout. Joseph had a good character of not fighting back or retaliating toward his enemies Imagine if it was you being framed/accused of wanting to rape the wife of your master, how far would you have gone, wanting to prove your innocence, how much would you have paid, looking for the best lawyers. Joseph just allowed himself to be arrested and sent to prison for a crime which he did not commit and I am sure he knew that in order for him to see his destiny he had to allow himself to go through the process. Great leaders do not cut corners in life; Joseph was certainly an example of a great leader.

If Joseph was not imprisoned he was not going to hear the dreams of the baker and cup bearer, in all of this, God was working and weaving His mysteries in the destiny of the young man Joseph. Madam Potiphar was not aware that the future governor of the country was the very one who had worked in their palace, she was not aware that she was sending Joseph to the road of his destiny. God works wonders, indeed His ways are not our ways. Joseph's destiny connector was right there in prison and if he had cut corners and bribed his way out of prison he was going to miss his destiny. Many of us have missed our destiny because we do not want to be subjected to harsh conditions in life. Do not always desire to be in a good position in life because you do not know where that will take you. The mystery of God was at work in Joseph's life from the day he was sold to the traders; he was not killed as was the initial plan by his brothers. We also see the greatness of God when he found himself face to face with a crisis of a lustful woman who wanted to take advantage of him because he was a slave. The hand of God upon Joseph continued even in prison when he was appointed a chief prisoner among other prisoners until, because of his trustworthy character the baker and the cup bearer came to him to share their dreams and by the grace and anointing of God upon his life he correctly interpreted the dreams. Joseph was a natural leader, leadership was innate.

After correctly interpreting the dreams of Pharaoh a big door opened for Joseph, not to be just an ordinary man but a powerful man in the nation of Egypt. I am sure that Joseph's brothers thought Joseph's dreams were only speaking of him to rule over them in Canaan hence the plot to kill him was contrived to see what came of his dreams. By selling him to the Ishmaelites, they thought they were killing his dreams. When God has declared a destiny in your life it will surely come to pass even if you are in prison like Joseph or when you are in another country. Maybe you have cried for many years thinking that things are not working where you are, but let me tell you, you might need a little shaking and moving away from your familiar environment to allow God to use you. Man of God you might have been failing to have a handful of people as members in your church, consult the Holy Spirit and move to another place for bigger room to enlarge your territory, spread your tent pegs. God uses people when they are in unfamiliar places where no one knows anything about them or their past. Joseph's destiny was in another nation but God had started revealing this when he was a very young man. This shows that God always makes sure that He fulfills His word even if the person involved is in another place. Moving away from your comfort zone can give God room to expand you, as a child of God opening your eyes to where and what you want in line with God's plans will enable you to grow. You no longer have customers in that business because everyone in that same area is selling the same products as you, pray to God to give you a new business idea or simply move away to new place and see the hand of God in your business.

The mysteries of God in Joseph's life made sure that a door for ruling was opened when he was a mere slave in Egypt, you will not understand the way God works. He was assigned to be a leader of other slaves, what you do when you are given a task can be your big breakthrough in your life. How many times have you been given something to do in your church or work place and you do it with such reluctance that no one will recommend you for promotion? When you want to go far in life execute all your given tasks with diligence.

After many years there was hunger in Canaan and the only available door to get food for survival was Egypt. They had forgotten the dreams which they had interpreted for the 17-year-old boy, that one day they will bow down in worship to this young man. They thought Joseph and his dreams were history, buried and forgotten. God had raised their brother's profile; he was now a respected man in a land which was not even his. God made sure that they come direct to the hands of Joseph and surprisingly they could not recognize him even though he had asked some personal questions about the welfare of their father and younger brother. People who do evil things to others seem to forget these things quickly. The dreams were being fulfilled years later in a foreign land, when God wants to bless you He does not wait to do it in a familiar place. Seriously selling Joseph to the Midianites was a major catalyst that sped up the achieving of his dreams; it was indeed a game changer in the whole mystery. You might be complaining that your boss or zone leader is giving you excessive loads of work and yet they are preparing a big promotion for you, just do what is required of you without complaining like Joseph did and see the end result. I know a group of people who were sent to evangelize and the group leader was assigning tasks to everyone without him doing anything at all, upon going back to church with results of many people giving their lives to Christ Jesus, the church leaders asked who preached the most and the leader mentioned all the names besides his and the people mentioned were all ordained evangelists and he was left out, such is the life of people who think they are using us not knowing they are propelling us to our destiny.

The same scenario took place when David was anointed King by Prophet Samuel. David was remembered by God when his father did not remember that he had a son in the field, today I pray that the same God will remember you for good in Jesus' Name, Amen!

Even the prophet himself at one point was looking at the outward appearance forgetting that God does not work with looks He works with those who have a willing heart. The Bible tell us that after David was anointed as King he went back to the wilderness and take care of the flock, I am sure waiting for his time to come. In life it is always good to wait for your time, not all of us arrive at our destiny at the same time. I can see the same characteristics in these two young men Joseph and David; they were humble and submissive to their fathers. I am sure David's father; mother and brothers thought a day will come whereby the young man will be declared king with a grand ceremony and momentous occasion. It took Jesse to ask the young man David instead of himself, to go and check on the welfare of his brothers at war. One can imagine how a grown up man like Jesse can ask a little boy to go and see how his brothers were faring in the battle with the Philistines. Only the mysteries of God can explain this because a stage was being set for the young man to announce his grand entry into the kingship which had been confirmed by the prophet years before. If David, like Joseph had refused to be sent to see how his brothers were doing it would have meant his destiny was going to be delayed or even ended. Obedience is always bigger and better than the sacrifices we make in life.

God set up a battle for David in order for King Saul and all the other Israelites to see what was in him; likewise, Joseph was sold by his brothers to his destiny. After defeating Goliath, it was all clear for everyone to see how powerful David was, the brave warrior he was in the nation of Israel. Sometimes you need a stage to be set up for you to be properly recognized. It seemed cruel when Jesse decided to send his younger son to war, but it was the right moment to make him shine and become prominent in the nation. So in life not all battles are there for you to die, some come hiding and yet will raise you up, when a stage is set for you, do your best because you do not know where it will take you. If your pastor gives you an opportunity to share the word of God during the time to sow in church, make sure that you do it so well that everyone will be compelled to give. If you are given time to close in prayer after a gathering do it with such anointing that people will see miracles from God through that prayer. God knew that David was an obedient child and allowed him to be sent to check on his brothers at war the same as what happened when Joseph was send to check on his brothers in the pastures.

If these two were stubborn and disobedient children of their parents, they would have missed their lifetime breakthroughs. I know this is a major lesson to some people who continuously disobey their leaders and parents, beware of missing what God has put in you because of seemingly small disobedience and stubbornness. Imagine missing a lifetime breakthrough just because of you missing church, skipping tithing and not reading the word of God. May God help us to realize the mysteries of God in our life. Saul missed the lifetime kingship for his generations because of disobedience, a simple mistake cost the whole generation their kingship. God works in mysterious ways that is His character, the way we think is not the way He thinks, he waits for a situation or a crisis to happen for Him to act.

Hannah was in a barrenness crisis and after so many years of crying to God for a child God acted at the right time and right moment. Our God is always on time. I believe you and I need a crisis for God to do major things in our lives. Do not run away from a crisis you need it for God to be seen and glorified. That is how God works. For us to testify about the greatness of God there should be a test to be passed, so crises are there to bring out the greatness of God in our lives. Peninah failed to understand the mysteries of God about Hannah's crisis, even in life we have people who laugh at others when they are in a calamity, forgetting that our God is a big God who is not afraid of any crisis. Let them laugh at you today because you do not have a job but soon your God will give you one, let them laugh at you because you are getting too old and not yet married or have a child do not worry my brother or my sister that is just a mystery that people are failing to understand. When God answers He does it in public to shame all who doubted the greatness of God upon your life. Remember destiny can be delayed but it will never be denied, everyone arrives at their own time.

What you are today is not how your life will be forever, what they see you as today is not what they will see you as in five years' time. The situation you are in today is not going to be the same situation you will be in next week these are the mysteries of God. What you are today can be a way to take you to the right position in your life, no one knows how life will be tomorrow for those people we are looking down upon today. You might be in a great position today but that does not mean you will be like that forever, tables might turn and the one who was ridiculed, the 'nobody', becomes somebody.

Teachers give birth to chief executive officers of big multinational companies, pilots, doctors and presidents and yet remain on that same level but God will always work mysteriously in everyone's life. Our destiny will never be the same no matter what, even if we are born by same mother and father our destiny will always be different. I am a testimony to this because I have been where none from my siblings had never been, I have many testimonies of this.

The same Nile river which the other young Hebrew boys were being thrown in to their death become the same river the baby Moses was hidden in and survived, you cannot understand how our heavenly God works. He orchestrated the mother of Moses to be paid to nurse her own son because God wanted to protect the boy for the deliverance of the Hebrews from Egyptian bondage. What a great and miraculous God we serve, that is a big mystery in a big crisis. The same Red Sea which swallowed the Egyptian army is the same Red Sea which gave way for the Hebrews and they walked on dry land leaning on the walls of water and no one got wet they all came out dry. The same palace which had declared death to the young Hebrew boys becomes the same palace Moses who was also a Hebrew called home. God works in a very mysterious manner, think of how He managed to take great care of the Israelites for 40 years in the wilderness. God made sure that the children of Israel never lacked anything in the wilderness until they reached the Promised Land.

Imagine people were growing with their clothes, and no clothes were torn, no one can explain this mystery, for 40 good years' no one needed a new set of shoes or clothes. Surely this can take a fool to not appreciate the greatness of God.

God can use the people you are taking out of problems to test your strength and mental stability as well. Moses needed to be mentally stronger to overcome the murmuring of the children of Israel he was leading out of Egypt to the Promised Land, the land of milk and honey. Do you know it is a big miracle that you can swallow food without problems, breathing in and out without the aid of a machine is a miracle, walking freely without the aid of a stick is a miracle because there are some people who want to walk on their own but they can't? The simultaneous blinking of your eyes is a miracle, a mystery that no one can explain besides God Himself. You need to love this

God; He can work something mysterious in your life without a doubt, which is His nature he will never fail.

It is important to know that as we are waiting on God for an answer to our prayers or if we are facing uncertainty that we have a powerful tool which is the word of God. Speak the word of God into every situation; this will keep you focused on Jesus the author and finisher of your faith! Doubt and discouragement will be far from you as you meditate on the powerful word of God.

CHAPTER 3

Reading the word of God, we see many stories where we witness that there are too many mysteries of God and you cannot finish them in one book. Every time God opened His mouth and say something it became a talking point, it became a miracle and a mystery. I am just talking of a few which without a doubt have allowed me to have no misgivings about the greatness of God. In this chapter I just want to talk about another mystery of God through another chilling incident which occurred in the region of Susa in the book of Ester. Sometimes when God wants to do big things He uses people of authority for it to make more sense. God knows that if he always uses people of no significance it cannot be news at all, for example the same shop you can go to everyday to buy food stuffs can be on the news headlines when Mesut Ozil goes to buy a bottle of water.

In this case God started by positioning the Savior first because He is an all knowing God who sees the future, like what He did by positioning Moses in the palace as a small boy to learn the palace language and then left when he was 40years only to come back when he was 80years old to deliver the Israelites from Egyptian bondage. We see here the same God positioned Esther in the palace through her uncle Mordecai who had taken her in as a little girl to live in Susa. One day when queen Vashti was demoted and sent packing from the palace because she had refused to strip naked in front of the King's delegates. This is because of the foolishness of the king who made decisions in his drunken state. When this happened Esther got the opportunity to be the next queen, because I believe all this was in the plans of God, that is why we always say God's plans are not like man's plans, we will never know what Gods next move is, you can never predict the next move of God.

I believe God knew what was to come and He wanted to make sure that the right person was in the palace as queen. Because of the king's foolish decisions which he was known for making when he was drunk he just listened to the enemy of the Jews in the name of Haman who wanted to destroy the whole Jewish tribe in Susa. The king endorsed that rule even without gathering all the facts, but because God was involved in the whole situation He was just waiting to show His superiority, because this is His mysterious way of doing things. Whenever people who hate you gather to plan evil for you as long God is on your side nothing will harm you, their evil plan will definitely fail. They can plan in private but God will embarrass them in public, this is exactly what happened with Haman he made his plan in private but the embarrassment was there for everyone to see, in public. Always be very careful of who you try to put down in private because the Lord God will embarrass you in public, making your shame a public display.

Esther 6:1-3: Mordecai Honored

1 That night the king could not sleep; so he ordered the book of the chronicles, the record of his reign, to be brought in and read to him. 2 It was found recorded there that Mordecai had exposed Bigthana and Teresh, two of the king's officers who guarded the doorway, who had conspired to assassinate King Xerxes. 3 "What

honor and recognition has Mordecai received for this?"
the king asked. "Nothing has been done for him," his
attendants answered.

The same God who made Ester and all the other people to
have sound sleep on one night made the King not to find
any sleep, thank God because of His mysterious ways of
doing things He caused the king not to ask for a singer or
a dancer or wine to be brought to him as was his custom.
Instead God made sure the king had to ask for the history
books to be brought to him to be read. I thank God because
of the librarian who was directed by God to pick the right
book at the right time. Hallelujah to Jesus Christ the son
of the living God! The moment the king saw it mentioned
in the book how Mordecai a Jew, a foreigner had exposed
the assassination plot by Bigthana and friends to eliminate
the king it immediately rang alarm bells in the mind of the
king. I am sure the librarian was not aware that what he
was reading had a big impact in the life of the Jews in the
region of Susa. Soon after the king heard about what
Mordecai did, the Bible tells us that he made up his mind

to give a reward to Mordecai the person who had done a very big thing in saving the life of the King.

In life when you do good things to other people even in private our God is so faithful to reward you in public in the eyes of everyone to see, even if people tend to forget what you might have done for them our God does not forget, this is exactly what happened to Joseph when the cup bearer forgot him when he got out of prison and was reinstated on his old position, he completely forgot about Joseph but when God's time came for Joseph to be useful in the whole land of Egypt God made sure that there was a dream which needed interpretation by Joseph. Our God does not sleep or slumber He is an all knowing God who does not forget things. Can I ask someone today, "What history do you have in your church, family or work place?" Do you think your name can appear in the history books of your family, church or country? If you do good deeds they will follow you and your generations that follow.

God knew that one day He would bring to the Kings' attention the noble deed of Mordecai did and it came at the right moment and right time where Haman had planned to eliminate the whole tribe of the Jews in Susa. The time the King heard about the heroics of Mordecai it so happened to be the same time Haman was coming to the king to finalize his plan of the destruction of Mordecai. Sometimes God make sure your enemies expose themselves in your absence without you fighting and defending yourself. Mordecai and the other Jews were busy praying to God to fight for them and the biggest enemy was also busy going to present himself to the king not knowing what was in store for him. When you fast and pray faithfully to God, He will always answer your prayers, God had caused the king to have a sleepless night in order to make him aware of what Mordecai had done. Do not worry, if you did not get your reward today it will surely come just keep doing good things even if there is no one clapping hands for you or seeing you. Our God is a faithful God He gives reward where it is deserved even if people have no plan to reward you.

Galatians 6 v 9

"And let us not be weary in well doing: for in due season, we shall reap if we faint not."

The king heard footsteps in the inner courtyard and when he asked who it was considering the time of the night he was told it was Haman. Haman was then asked by the king what can be done to the person whom the king delighted to honor, in his mind Haman thought there was no one the king would want to honor besides him, he was self-centered and he mentioned all the good things he wanted the king to do for him little did he know that he was talking about someone else who he considered his enemy. The mystery of God caused him speak promotion to the person he wanted to destroy! Hallelujah to Jesus, may God cause your enemies to speak and declare your promotion, in Jesus mighty name!

God can lead those people who hate you to speak about your promotion, our God is so faithful He works in ways we cannot see and He makes a way for us where there seems to be no way. Haman thought the moment of his promotion had come but he was unaware that it was his time of destruction had come. The same gallows he had made thinking they are for Mordecai turned out to be for himself, he unknowingly built his own hanging place. God will always bring shame to those people who continuously plan horror for us. He always puts the evil people to shame with their evil ways. The devil is a big liar and a failure as long we know who we are in Christ and have our relationship with God intact.

After all the declarations Haman had made he was left with mud on his face when he was told by the king to go at once to do all that he had said to Mordecai the Jew. I can imagine the level of embarrassment he faced, the pain he felt from inside and the shame he had. You can't fight with God's people and win, never, you will definitely bite the dust, and God will embarrass you. That is how our God operates, He is a mysterious God, and He does things in a mysterious way. He operated against the laws which were made, the Jews were allowed to defend themselves and it was for the first time in the book of Esther that the king had made a good decision, praise be to God. A person who was like a slave turned out to be a person of authority Mordecai became a governor in a foreign land just like

Joseph in Egypt, he became in charge of the region and yet he was a foreigner. When God opens a door no one can close it, and when He closes a door no one can open it. When He says yes no one can say no, and when He say no, no one has the power to say yes,

Mordecai's time had come for promotion, a reward which he deserved, unlike Haman who wanted a position out of evil doing. Sometimes what is delaying your rightful position is what you do when you are given an opportunity to shine. You might be surprised that the person you are despising today or the one who you are busy planning evil against is the one to propel you to your position of influence. When position seems not to locate you at your place of birth move away and go somewhere surely God will bless you there.

The same king in the book of Nehemiah who had taken the Jews to bondage is the same person God used to give orders for Nehemiah to be offered all the diplomatic benefits on his way back to Jerusalem to rebuild the city's broken walls. Never underestimate the power of God in your life it is never too late for Him to do something great in your life. God can turn your enemies into companions; He can command your enemies to be on your side, to be the ones who can assist you one day. That is how mysterious our God is, you cannot predict His way of doing things. Who would have thought that in the book of Nehemiah, Nehemiah would be given a diplomatic letter by King Artaxerxes who was using him as a slave in exile? Your enemies can be turned by God to help you; this is how God can turn tables in our lives. That person who is hurting you today can be used by God to propel you to the position of influence, and sometimes they do it unawares that they are doing good.

Who would have thought that when Samaria was under siege in 2 Kings 6 and 7 when people were eating one another, that the deliverance of the whole city was lying in the hands of the four lepers who were considered outcasts and write offs. Remember these four were now living outside the city because the laws stated that they should be outcasts, but they did not know that one day the same outcasts would save the whole nation. In so many cases we think that some people are useless but it turns out that those are the ones who will be used by God as our point of contact for victory.

How many times have you been embarrassed when you see someone whom you looked down upon at some time now in a position of influence? Imagine seeing a boy you used to ridicule as the chief executive officer of a major institution. God can change people and their situations, what you are seeing in me today is not what you will see of me in the next five years. Ultimately, being an outcast like the four lepers is not the end of the world for you. God can use you in that state of being an outcast. When people write you off do not despair as long you know God is on your side nothing will happen to you. No weapon formed against you shall prosper. When people throw you out of their lives and turn their backs on you because of a crisis cheer up and get ready to shine, the same people will definitely celebrate you the next day when God has lifted you up.

I can go on and on mentioning the mysteries of God in a crisis in the Bible and in the lives of many people. I just mentioned the ones which touched my life. Where have you seen a crisis in your life and God's greatest and mighty hand gave you victory? Without a crisis God does not work, in other words a crisis allows our God to become active.

One has to be in a crisis of sickness for our God to be seen as a healer, someone has to be in a barren crisis like Hannah for God to be seen opening the womb of that person, someone has to be in a crisis of blindness like Bartmius before the hand of God is seen as that person is prayed for and their sight is restored. There has to be a bad situation for a miracle to be seen. It took Hannah's barrenness for God to silence Peninnah and other people who were laughing at her because of barrenness. It needed a Samuel to be given to God by his mother Hannah for Eli the priest to have a successor, hallelujah.

Judges 13:2-5

2 A certain man of Zorah, named Manoah, from the clan of the Danites, had a wife who was childless, unable to give birth. 3 The angel of the Lord appeared to her and said, "You are barren and childless, but you are going to become pregnant and give birth to a son. 4 Now see to it that you drink no wine or other fermented drink and that you do not eat anything unclean. 5 You will become pregnant and have a son whose head is never to be touched by a razor because the boy is to be a Nazirite, dedicated to God from the womb. He will take the lead in delivering Israel from the hands of the Philistines."

Manoah and his wife were barren and God heard their prayers and blessed them with a son whom they named Samson and it is how God brought a redeemer for Israel through this child Samson. As children of God a crisis is what determines our God's superiority, grace and favour.

When Jesse and his wife were looking for outward looks for a possible king in their family God was looking for the one who was small but with a kingly anointing inside of him. What matters most was what God had ordained in David, the one after the heart of God. The whole camp of the Israel army including King Saul was afraid of the giant Goliath who ridiculed them for 40 days but when God wants to intervene he will use a David, the least, that is His nature. When Jesse sent David to check up on his brothers' maybe he knew that in David was a small package with big explosives and his time to shine had arrived. Just think again, what caused David to be at the camp of the Israelites army at the right time when Goliath was undertaking his usual stance mocking the God of Israel together with the armies of Israel? Remember David's anointing was done in front of only his family members but the confirmation was for the whole city to witness. Seriously this is all because of the mysteries of God; He made sure He positioned David where he was needed the most. He made sure David was at a place where his ascending to kingship was guaranteed. Others were using sharp weapons but David needed a smooth stone to defeat the Philistine warrior who had on full armor. Israel was delivered by a mere young man but whom God had ordained to lead his people. When God is on your side nothing will harm you or have the power to raise his hand against you. In all the battles you might be facing in life you just need the hand of God to be upon your life and it will give you victory.

There was no need for David to use heavy artillery to win the war he used what God had directed, even when Saul tried to give him his armor and clothes for war they did not fit on the young David. Not all clothes for war fit everyone; this shows us that levels of battles may differ with people in life.

God always positions His people at the right place and at the right time. The Shunamite woman was barren but God sent her the anointed servant of God Elisha to come and lodge at her house to unlock her womb. If she had not welcomed Prophet Elisha and his servant Gehazi she was not going to witness her miracle. What is causing your unfruitfulness can be destroyed when you minister to servants of God. The Zarephath widow was delivered from poverty and hunger because God sent a hungry prophet Elijah to her home. The same as the widow who was the wife of one of the dead sons of the prophets, she was delivered from the looming bondage of her sons just because of the positioning of the man of God in the city. She has to know where to run to with her problems and that unlocked her breakthrough, from being poor to being a business woman selling oil in her city because of the anointing of a servant of God prophet Elisha. You need to have spiritual eyes to see the servants of God around you. The Shunamite woman had eyes to see that prophet Elisha was in the city and so she provided for him and his servant, the widow of Zarephath did the same when prophet Elijah was passing by and she and her son were saved from hunger. How many times have you prayed for a miracle and yet never that by looking after servants of God around you can unlock your breakthrough and receive a miracle?

Our God sees the future He is omnipotent, what we do not see now or ahead, He sees. When we do not see the outcome of every situation He knows the solution and the results in advance. When the sons of the prophets decided that they needed a bigger place to live they asked Elisha for company and when one's exe head fell in the water it took the mystery of God to use His servant to make it float against human understanding and science. Some of us do not even want servants of God near us even when we are venturing in to other missions we avoid servants of God but when problems arise along the way it is easy to get the spiritual covering because the servant of God is there with you. Even if you are going for a big business meeting ask the servant of God to intercede for you as you undertake the meetings.

Involving a servant of God in your day to day programs represents the presence of God that is why you see that all the battles in the word of God were fought when there is a priest who was involved meaning priests represent the presence of God. When a problem arises and you are far from the servant of God and you had not even told him to pray for you before you started the journey. When the pot of soup turned to poison God used His servant to pour flour in it to be edible. Another mystery of God in a crisis is when the only son of that Shunamite woman died, God came through His servant to bring the boy back to life, imagine if that Shunamite woman had behaved the way most of us do towards servants of God who are around us, what would have been the end result of her son. These are just few incidents I have mentioned but there are many recorded in the Bible as well as in our everyday lives. It takes the greatness of God for one to be balanced when walking because some people cannot walk without the aid of a stick hallelujah.

God works in extremely miraculous ways, in as much as we know He is capable of doing miracles, the how part is so very unpredictable. We might predict the outcome but how it is done we cannot predict. God can use anyone anywhere as long it fulfills His will. Jonah decided to run away from the work of God but God used a whale to swallow him for three days and three nights and he was spewed out to his destination. God can use anything in this world to fulfill His purpose that is why He used a whale to transport Jonah, just think of how he was breathing inside the whale for three days and three nights. Have you ever thought of why Jonah was not digested by this whale, what happened to the digestive system of the whale for three days and three nights? Can someone explain how Jonah was being fed inside the whale, who can tell me how he relieved himself while he was inside the whale, all these are questions which we cannot answer? Only God can do what no man can do in our lives. God does not worry about the how part in our journey of life; he is only concerned with who to use in order to fulfill His plans.

I remember one day when I was travelling from Zimbabwe, Harare to Malawi Lilongwe I missed the bus which was supposed to take me direct to Lilongwe without passing through Blantyre. God allowed me to oversleep and I woke up very late. I became so angry because I knew how taxing the journey was. I do not even know how everyone in the house missed the alarm. Out of frustration I went to catch a bus to Blantyre with the option of catching up with that direct bus to Lilongwe at the Zimbabwe and Mozambique border. On arriving at Nyamapanda border I asked immigration officers if the bus was still far, they informed me it had just passed the border. After I arrived at Mozambique border I was told I had missed the bus by 10min, and I became so angry and exasperated. After we had travelled some distance just after the Mozambique town called Tete I saw dark smoke in front of us. When we arrived at the scene which was the source of the smoke we discovered that it was the bus which I had missed, it apparently caught fire from nowhere, thank God there were no casualties but I heard that people had lost all their luggage they could not be salvaged from the fire. Imagine if I had woken up on time and caught that bus, all my luggage would have been burnt in that bus or who knows maybe I would have been the only casualty. The lesson here is in so many cases we rush to conclusion and yet it is God himself who would have saved us. The bus burnt beyond recognition but thank God no one was hurt. I have heard many cases where people involved in a car crash were not injured but the car was damaged beyond repair, that is what we call the mysteries of God. Have you ever thought about the same headache which did not kill you is the same headache which is killing someone else right now? Surely it is very difficult to predict the works of God.

One of my friends, a Pastor whose wife gave birth in the car on their way to the hospital without any aid from nurses or doctors and yet nothing bad happened to the mother and the child, but also I know of some people whose wives cannot give birth without involvement of specialists because of complications, or many who died giving birth in front of all the nurses and doctors maybe because it might be their time to die. Our God works in a very strange way yet very miraculously. You and I sometimes need a crisis in our lives for us to see the great hand of God. What you are afraid of might be that which God wants to use to show the whole world His greatness.

Chapter Four

In this chapter I will talk about many other works and testimonies of God in the Bible and in life. Some of the testimonies I will share I have experienced firsthand and others were experienced by people in ministry. In the book of 1st and 2nd Kings we read about the two great servants of God, Prophet Elijah the Tishbite and his predecessor prophet Elisha who had been used mightily by God. I will touch some incidences where there were major crises and God was seen through His servants. In 1 Kings 17 we see conflict between Elijah and King Ahab and this lead to the servant of God declaring that there will be no rain or dew for three and half years in the land, that was a prophecy or declaration for drought in the land. I strongly believe prophet Elijah did not make this declaration just for fun but he said it in order to prove to King Ahab and his wife Jezebel that he is a servant of God and the same God who used him mightily. Notice how God operates especially through His called ones, when a servant of God opens his/her mouth and speaks things happen, never underestimate the power of the words which come from the mouth of the servants of God around you or in your life. I always tell fellow servants of God that we need to be very careful of what we speak to our members and people around us because the anointing we carry is powerful and if we are not careful we might end up use that anointing to speak evil into our members' lives.

1 Kings 17:1: New International Version

Elijah Announces a Great Drought

17 Now Elijah the Tishbite, from Tishbe[a] in Gilead, said to Ahab, "As the Lord, the God of Israel, lives, whom I serve, there will be neither dew nor rain in the next few years except at my word."

Elijah declared that there will be no rain for three and half years and the heavens heard him because of the great anointing he was carrying. Ahab took this lightly because he did not understand spiritual protocol and the great anointing which was on Prophet Elijah. Ahab and his whole kingdom experienced this drought for the period which the servant of God had declared and it took the same servant of God to get down on his knees in prayer to command rains to return to the land. From a serious drought throughout the whole land to abundance of rain that is how our mighty God operates and if you do not have any relationship with Him you might fail to understand His mysteries when there is a crisis.

You might be in a valley in your life where things seem like they are not working or moving. Or you might be facing a drought in areas of finances, your business is not operating the way you expected or planned or your marriage may be facing problem after problem, but I want to assure you that when God through His servants speaks there will be an abundance of rain in your life. You will have an abundance of testimonies. That is why I always encourage people to make sure that they are under the covering of a servant of God so that God can speak to your life through them. Spiritual covering is crucial in the life of a child of God. Do not forget the case of the Shunamite woman I mentioned before, no valley or situation in anyone's life can be too deep before God. What you just need to do is to make sure that God is involved and that will guarantee your victory.

Do not be comfortable when you live a life of not having a servant of God or priest who speaks blessings upon your life, which is very dangerous. There is a devil out there who always seeks to disturb our lives and with the covering of servants of God you will be protected. Going to church is not doing anyone but yourselves a favour, reading the word of God is not a waste of time or fasting and praying on your own is not a sign of being foolish or poor, it is actually good for you and your family. You might see it as time wasting but let me tell you when calamity strikes that is when you realize that you need a servant of God in your life. When Elijah feared for his life because of Ahab and his evil wife Jezebel he went and hid near the brook Cherith. Again we see God coming into play with His everlasting power; our Heavenly Father will never run out of miracles. In every situation He can brew an enormous miracle and that will leave many people in shock.

1 Kings 17:2-6: New International Version

Elijah Fed by Ravens

2 Then the word of the Lord came to Elijah: 3 "Leave here, turn eastward and hide in the Kerith Ravine, east of the Jordan. 4 You will drink from the brook, and I have directed the ravens to supply you with food there." 5 So he did what the Lord had told him. He went to the Kerith Ravine, east of the Jordan, and stayed there. 6 The ravens brought him bread and meat in the morning and bread and meat in the evening, and he drank from the brook.

When Elijah went to the brook Cherith I am sure he was not aware that the great I AM would reveal Himself as Jehovah Rapha which means the Lord who provides for His own. He ate fresh warm meat twice a day, and take note of the messenger God used to provide this meat for him. God commanded a raven of all the birds of the sky to provide food for Elijah. A raven is a bird which feeds on anything including meat as and God used it to bring fresh meat to Prophet Elijah without a piece missing. Some of us cannot be faithful with what God has given us to share. Do you think God would have left the raven hungry when it was being used to feed the servant of God, definitely not? The reason why you might be poor or hungry today is because you are not faithful in the eyes of God, whenever you are blessed with anything you do not share with the less privileged. Begin to share what you have and God will keep providing for you for the rest of your life. When God wants to perform a miracle He uses anything that is available so make sure that you are that available vessel for God to use you. You might be the next available vessel God is looking to use to perform miracles at your work place, church or community or even in your family but your character might be the limitation.

The Bible tells us that he would eat and satisfied and drink from the brook Cherith while everyone else in the kingdom was looking for water to drink. God will never leave you unsatisfied, He provides in full and just as in the Prophet Elijah's life. God will never send you where He will not provide, that is not His nature. The problem most of us have is that we do not trust in this God, we seem to doubt Him. God knows your future, you are where you are today and I can tell you that it was God's plans, and He knew exactly what you will eat, where you will sleep and everything you desire. Nothing in your life happens by accident, your marriage is not by accident it is God who has directed you to your spouse even though you might not be satisfied with them, even the children you have are not a mistake, no one comes to this earth by mistake, everything happens according to God's plan. Do not look down upon what God has given you He knows you are the best custodian who knows how to handle what He has given you for your future. The same child you might be calling a mistake today can grow up and be the greatest person in your country while those you feel came because of your plans might not do great in life. Giving birth to children means you are just a vessel God is using to fulfill His promises in the word of God.

1 Kings 17:8-9: New International Version

8 Then the word of the Lord came to him: 9 "Go at once to Zarephath in the region of Sidon and stay there. I have directed a widow there to supply you with food."

When the brook dried up God directed Elijah to the widow of Zarephath so that he could survive again, God does not look at your status in the community when He wants to perform a miracle. Many who are reading this would have argued and asked what a poor widow could give you during a season of drought. How many times have you missed your miracle or breakthrough just because you looked down upon the person carrying that miracle? I am sure several of us even look down upon ourselves as not being the right candidates to be used by God but as long you believe in God you can be used in any situation. Being a widow, orphan or disabled cannot limit you from being used by God. God can use you in the same way he can use the rich the married and the able bodied. Disability is not inability; you have your own unique way of doing things in this world. Imagine yourself in the shoes of Prophet Elijah seeing the ravens come to you with fresh meat, how were you going to react? Or if God had directed you to the widow were you not going to ask question after question? Elijah knew the way God works so he was obedient in every instruction that was given by God. When you have a strong relationship with God and know how He works you will always be ready to see any kind of miracle. Most of us miss our miracles because we are always looking for bigger stages to witness our great breakthroughs we overlook the small things which we deem useless and yet they carry mighty outcomes. Someone reading this might be afraid of birds and when you are dying of hunger and you see a bird bringing fresh meat you react in fear and chase away your miracle all because of fear. Most people have allowed fear to reign in their lives and thereby limiting what God wants to do in their lives.

Out of all the people in the land God looked for a faithful person to use, and in this case the widow of Zarephath. It is the grace of God to be found a faithful person. God is not using you to perform miracles because of reasoning too much or being unfaithful. When you want God to touch your life do not reason because that might hinder God from performing what He wants to in your life or even in other people's lives. In as much as it was difficult for the widow she did not reason or use logic she simply complied. The widow could have begun to explain her way out of blessing the servant of God prophet Elijah, she could have told him about the drought, about how her husband passed away, that she was a widow and that he would be better off going to a married couple. Many people would have even begun to feel sorry for themselves desiring to obtain sympathy from the servant of God.

Do not be hindered from receiving your breakthroughs in life by your stance in the area of giving. I tell business people that how they react when they receive large sums of money is stopping them from receiving their first million dollars. Are you mature enough to be faithful with your tithe of a million dollars today? Do you think God will trust you with millions of dollars when you cannot be faithful with very small amounts? God uses people who are faithful in giving and tithing and he blesses them to live in abundance because He knows that they know how to use money responsibly. I pray that God would enable you to be a worthy vessel to be used in order to connect with your destiny. The widow of Zarephath was good at tapping in to this anointing and God found her to be the most faithful candidate to allow His greatness to be perceived. Are you a good candidate for God to use to feed a servant of God in your city?

When Elijah approached the widow as she was gathering a few sticks to prepare her last meal to eat with her son, he asked for water first. Look how God operates, Elijah knows that there is drought in the land and he is asking a woman to give him water. Whenever we want to unlock blessings we need to seed or give what we love the most. Remember this was a season where there was no water in the land and how this widow managed to have water in her house is a big mystery. For the widow to receive a blessing of food she had to give the prophet food and she received an everlasting supply from God. If you want money seed money, if you want children seed a child like what Hannah did when she gave birth to Samuel. Abraham did the same when he gave birth to Isaac and today we are all here as children of Abraham by faith. It was normal for the widow to stand her ground and refuse to give Prophet Elijah water or even a bun but because she knew the importance of giving she submitted. God operates in a way which does not use force; He wants us to be free in decision making.

Elijah did not have to preach to this woman in order to convince her to give like what most of us need today, someone has to read the scriptures for us to be moved to give. Giving is something that should come from our hearts we should not to be pushed. When you give God sees your heart. If you still need someone to coerce you into doing what is right you are lost and you will not enjoy the goodness of God's kingdom.

God sometimes operates in strange methods; He can ask you for what is extremely valuable to you in order to give you more. He did this to Abraham when He asked him to give Him his only son which he had received in his old age, the son of promise Isaac. The moment Abraham accepted the challenge he triggered the heavens and mystery came into play. If Abraham had refused to give the son of promise Isaac, as a sacrifice God would have never provided the lamb. Would you surrender to God that which you value most, would you obey without reasoning and asking questions? When you value something so much give it to God and you will receive more of that from Him. I thank God the widow had water in her house because as she was going to fetch it she heard the servant of God ask for bread too. Maybe of all the things in the widow's house at that moment the water was not a problem to give so she might have hurriedly wanted to get rid of the servant of God with water and off he goes. The whole miracle process started when she agreed to give the servant of God water which I believe was also very precious during that time when the whole region was facing serious drought. How many times do we miss the chance to receive more from God when we refuse to give Him the little we have? Sometimes we think this God is cruel but that is how He operates; He asks little from us in order to give us bigger portions. This was too much for the widow hence she said I only have a handful of flour in a jar and little oil which I want to bake and eat with the boy and die, but Elijah instead of feeling sorry for her he continued to say just do as I said and see the hand of God, there will be abundance in your house in the season of drought. The Bible tells us that after Elijah ate from the widow's provision the little oil and handful of flour she had, never ran out during the whole season of drought. She lived in abundance in a season of drought; you can live in abundance wherever you are when others are dying with hunger if you are connected with the servants of God. The Bible also tells us about Isaac who sowed in a time of drought and he was blessed.

Genesis 26 v 12 NKJV

Then Isaac sowed in that land, and reaped in the same year a hundredfold; and the LORD blessed him.

The reason why some of us seem not to be progressing in life is because when God avails an opportunity to bless us we turn it down by reasoning or by failing to see that this is an opportunity which God has availed to us in order to take us to another level of life. As children of God when an opportunity to tap in to the anointing comes we need to grab it and receive the blessing, stop asking useless questions, just do it immediately and see if God will not live to fulfill His word upon your life. God provided for the widow and the little boy throughout the whole season of lacking. You are lacking some things today because you failed to grab an opportunity to give to the servants of God when it came so that you receive more. One of our biggest mistakes is to make unnecessary consultations to the wrong people when we want to do things in the house of God, for servants of God or even just giving anyone in our surroundings. The widow did not go and ask her relatives or neighbours for advice about what the prophet had said, she believed the words of the servant of God and acted upon them. I made it a policy in my to never not consult people on giving because how I received the conviction to give is not how the people I am consulting have heard. If you want to go very far in life never involve people who are on a lower level of spirituality in spiritual matters. When your heart is being convicted to give go for it and do what God is saying to you. I remember several times when I was convicted to give to God I would just do so without even consulting my wife or children because I do not want to disturb the move of the Holy Spirit in the whole process. I ended up teaching my family that when they hear God on something they must not hesitate to pray and do it instantly without delay. We do not have problem in the area of giving as a family; we have given things in the house of God from household furniture, clothes, money, cars and even food and ourselves to the work of God. I know of a widow in my home country who is so faithful and obedient in the area of giving. She is a blessing to many servants of God and she always declares that she is a well of water to those who are thirsty and a raven to those who are hungry. She is blessed beyond measure because of how influential she is to so many servants of God. She pays school fees for children of the servants of God in her area, she takes care of widows and orphans in her neighborhood and yet she is also a widow. He secret is that when her husband died several years ago she purposed tin her heart to go crazy in giving because she said she did not want to lack anything. Surely this widow is blessed she lacks nothing just because she unlocked her breakthroughs because of giving in abundance to servants of God.

Chapter Five:

Life Testimonials

A testimony is commonly referred to as a specific event in a Christian's life in which God did something deemed particularly worth sharing to encourage someone about the greatness of God. I love the part, 'deemed particularly worth sharing', meaning the one who is sharing has seen that his testimony is worth sharing with others. So in this chapter I want to share more of real life testimonies which I have personally experienced and some I have witnessed them from my friends and brothers in ministry. Sometimes in life you need to acknowledge the anointing and testimonies of other people and fellow servants of God just to show that there is unity in the kingdom. Personally I appreciate and recognize the level of calling upon other servants of God. Remember we are all anointed and called differently and we should therefore complement one another in their areas of gifting. Remember that in this book I am bringing out the mysteries of God in a crisis and different ones of cause, because what is a testimony to someone might not be a testimony to another. Someone might be thanking God because of a slice of bread while that might be nothing to a child whose father is a baker, living in a house cannot be a testimony to someone who is a builder, or wearing new clothes might not be a testimony to a child of a tailor. Therefore, what can be viewed as a crisis by someone in another community and culture might not be a crisis to someone from a different background. So to help the reader understand and appreciate this chapter, I sincerely plead with you not to judge or ridicule someone else's testimony. God is seen in different ways and beliefs depending on your point of view. People see God differently when they face problems; they see Him from their own perspective. We all come from different backgrounds, cultures and languages, so our belief in the way God does miracles differs. Remember a testimony to Hannah when she finally gave birth to Samuel was nothing in the eyes of Peninah because she had many children without problems. Also remember I am coming from an African background where some of the things we call testimonies might not be testimonies to people from the western world/overseas. Therefore, I encourage the reader to get the whole message this book is driving home which is to bring out the greatness of God in a crisis or critical situation in our lives.

Someone from a church that one of my friends is leading approached this pastor on a Saturday afternoon with the sad news that her three brothers were suddenly struck with blindness without any medical explanation. The servant of God prayed for the three blind brothers over the phone since they were far from where they were gathering and nothing happened. The following day on a Sunday during a deliverance session in church with the same servant of God who prayed, prayed again for the blind men, this time with their pictures being shown on the mobile phone. As the servant of God was praying evil spirits started manifesting on the sister of these blind brothers who had brought this prayer request, the demons were saying that they want to kill the three brothers, but because their sister had brought their prayer request to the pastor they felt the heat and let them go. The servant of God cast out the evil spirits in Jesus' Name and immediately the three blind brothers received their sight. They called their sister straight away and told her the good news that their sight had been restored. Shame on the devil because our God has no boundaries and He is not limited because of distance.

We have seen in the Bible when a centurion came to Jesus Christ requesting prayer for his sick servant even without Jesus having to touch him. *Luke 7 vs 1-10*. Our God is not limited to distance. By having faith, you can receive your healing, even by just reading this book. Miracles are not limited by distance they can happen anytime from anywhere, imagine all three brothers receiving their sight after prayers by a servant of God who was very far away from them. Do not be afraid to call a servant of God to share your problem and be prayed for and surely as you believed and have faith in God surely a miracle will be seen happening to you.

In 2014 I was invited to preach at a certain conference. I prepared by praying and fasting for a week that God would use me mightily. The day came and I started off to the conference on a Thursday morning. I was the one opening the first service that evening. On the way we found the bridge overflowing and it was impossible to drive through.

The bus driver told us that if the water level did not recede it would be risky to cross. The place was remote there were no shops or lodges where people could buy food or sleep. Even the mobile network was down. I could not communicate with anyone back home or even update the host of the conference. It was now midday, we had spent over four hours at the river and it was still raining heavily. As I was praying while seated in the bus the Holy spirit encouraged me to go and step into the edge of the flooded river near the bridge and pray for the water level to go down. Immediately, I asked for an umbrella and went to the bridge, I stepped knee high into the water and began praying, commanding the water level to drop. As soon as I finished praying the water level began to go down rapidly so that the bridge was now left clear for any driver to see, remember it was raining heavily. Everyone in the bus and other cars were surprised and people began to celebrate by hooting as they crossed the flooded river. We crossed safely and I was the topic of conversation in the bus, people gave me offerings and some brought their prayer requests so that I could pray for them.

When I arrived at the conference I sensed that there would be serious miracles that would take place. The moment I stepped on to the podium to preach I was loaded with the anointing. I preached and prayed for the people. As I was closing for the night I gave two prophetic words as follows

1. There is a woman who has a cancerous wound which is not healing. I mentioned that she had been from doctor to doctor with no change, that her health was actually deteriorating and that she was embarrassed because of the putrid odor emanating from the wounds. I declared that by tomorrow the wound would be totally dry and healed. I did not know the woman and this took place in a foreign country where I was a total stranger.

2. I also said that God had shown me a young girl in hospital with a fractured leg. I declared that she was healed right now and that tomorrow her parents will bring her to the conference. I then prayed for both prophecies and closed the session and I was ushered to my hotel.

The following day I was picked up for morning service and as soon as I arrived at the conference venue while our car was being parked a certain woman rushed to the car and lifted up her dress to show everyone that the cancerous wound had miraculously healed. Ushers were trying to cover her but she did not want all that, she exclaimed that she had shown too many doctors her wound because she wanted healing so why not show a man of God and congregants a miracle like this!

As we were in the service when everyone was thanking God for the healing of this lady, the host pastor received a call. He answered it because it was the church administrator who was not in attendance because he had gone to see his daughter in hospital who was admitted because of a fractured leg! Are you getting something here? The pastor jumped after hearing the voice of the administrator. He screamed, "hallelujah to Jesus", as he went and grabbed the microphone from the praise and worshipper who was singing and motioned for her to keep quiet. He then announced that the daughter of the administrator was discharged because doctors had no idea how she was healed before they had even put a cast on her. Now I understood that the river was flooded because the devil wanted to delay the miracles, the prophetic and healing words for these two people. God showed up at the right time in a place where I was a complete stranger. Hallelujah to our God!

Another testimony is that of my daughter, when she was about eleven months old one morning she just cried out loud and collapsed. We rushed her to the hospital in our neighbor's car. On the way we were praying and also called my Archbishop to pray for her. Upon arriving at the medical facility the doctors and nurses rushed to conduct some tests and to their surprise they could not find anything wrong with her. They tested everything but nothing abnormal was found, remember she was not moving or breathing. The main reason we had rushed to the hospital quickly was because there was an outbreak of typhoid and the government through the ministry of health had issued a statement that any mysterious symptoms or sickness should be quickly reported to medical facilities. We heard them whispering to each other that she is dead and they did not want us to know or hear what they were saying. I immediately asked them to give me back the child and they said all sorts of things discouraging me not to do that but I insisted and I asked my wife to put the motionless child on her back and start walking back home because our neighbor had gone already he was rushing to his business. To the surprise of the medical staff we left and went home with a literally dead baby on my wife's back. We decided to walk back home so that we can have enough time to pray as we were walking. We started praying for life for the child and we prayed like mad people along the way home. When you are embarrassed to pray in public it means the situation is still good on your side. When the situation looks dangerous you can pray anytime anywhere without worrying about what other people that are looking at you will say. If you know that you want to get married you will be no respecter of people you can even pray and speak in tongues in a bus, train or aero plane full of people. Prayer is talking to God and when the situations calls for it you can pray anywhere and anytime.

My Archbishop and his wife were also on their way to our house. When we arrived home we continued praying and I could see that my wife had tears streaming down her face but she did not want me to see. After a few minutes the child sneezed twice and cried again and started asking for milk. My wife rushed to the fridge to get a bottle of milk, she gave her a cup of milk and my daughter began to sweat profusely. After drinking the milk, she immediately stood up and off she went outside to play as if nothing had happened. We were left speechless; we could not laugh or talk we just thanked our God. For over three hours she was motionless and we thought she was dead. Those who know our daughter as a young child know that she was hyper active, even now she is like that, she cannot sit in one place for a longtime. Even when my Archbishop and mama arrived they were surprised to see her with her doll, playing outside looking good as if nothing had happened to her. We narrated everything to them and they prayed again thanking God for her life and good health. I am not saying the medical people could not do their job well, I still value them up to this day because they were used to tell us that the child is dead and that pushed us to pray. I really feel the sickness was more of a spiritual attack than just an ordinary sickness. Even when you are sick today seek spiritual covering first and then go to the medical facility and receive proper guidance and treatment by people who are qualified to do that, but sometimes spiritual things need people like servants of God who can fight or do their job in the spiritual aspect or point of view. Some situations need stubborn faith and also give God room for a miracle to happen, remember crisis comes in different ways.

Another testimony is that of a couple who wanted a child as they had not conceived after six years of marriage and there was no sign of even a miscarriage. They had visited all the specialists and they were told that the wife had a problem and they will never have a child unless they adopt one. They constantly updated their servants of God about all the doctors were saying and prayer and fasting were done, after some time of being faithful in prayer and fasting the couple were told good news that the wife had conceived and this really surprised the doctors. You see, sometimes our problems cannot be solved or explained by science of this world, it only takes God Himself to come to our rescue and to know exactly how to solve our problems. The servants of God did not stop praying and when the time of delivery came and the doctors told them that the only way she can give birth is by having an operation/C-section. They again notified their pastor who kept praying for her and one day they visited her in the hospital ward and they found the husband already there signing the papers for the doctors to proceed with the operation, but just as the servant of God and his wife were praying the birth pains increased and the child started to push and they were asked to leave the ward. They continued praying while outside the hospital ward and within a few minutes the woman had a normal delivery without any complications, both the child and the mother were healthy. Hallelujah to Jesus Christ of Nazareth.

The doctors were, for a long time, amazed by such miracles and they could not understand how it happened. I am not telling fairytales or that I just want to be relevant, I know and understand the power of God whom II serve. I personally know the couple I am talking about. Miracles are still and will forever happen and if they are yet to be seen in your life keep praying and have faith in your heavenly God one day you will see what I am talking about and you will surely testify. Our God is a miracle worker and way maker. Miracles did not only occur in the time of Moses when he witnessed a talking, burning bush, in the time of Elisha and Elijah the prophets or during times of Jesus Christ. Miracles did not end in the Bible, no they are still happening today. I pray that you receive a miracle of whatever you need, right now in Jesus' mighty Name.

When we receive the doctor's diagnosis it only means we now know what to pray for. I will say this again; when you are sick you should seek spiritual covering first and then proceed to the doctors. We need the medical people in our life they guide us and confirm some of these miracles as well, may the dear Lord God bless them, but it is also important to know your background and the type of demons you have to fight.

Another family lost their daughter for over a day she just disappeared and it was not in her nature to do that, they called a man of God whom I also know and they asked him to pray for their daughter to be found alive and safe. The servants of God prayed with the family throughout the night and the following morning around 5am they received a call that the daughter was found in a nearby town and she was in the hands of police because she was kidnapped and she managed to escape in the night as the kidnappers were drunk and they both fell into a deep sleep. She told the police that she had overheard the kidnappers talking about taking turns to rape her. Look how important it is to involve servants of God in your problems because you are covered in prayers and you are protected because they carry an anointing upon their lives. Who knows if they had not called the servant of God to seek Godly guidance what would have happened to their daughter?

I strongly believe that the prayers throughout the night, triggered the power of our heavenly Father to make the kidnappers go into a deep sleep so that they could not hear the girl escaping. In the word of God in 1 Samuel 9 we see a boy Saul going to the man of God to ask for the whereabouts of donkeys, how much more about a beloved daughter's whereabouts! When you are in a problem knowing where to go to is the most important thing in life of a child and believer of God. This testimony encourages me to put God first in every situation, if its sickness we put God first and then leave everything in the hands of the doctors to do the physical job and if it is a case like this of a kidnapped daughter we call upon the name of our heavenly Father in prayer and leave the rest to the law enforcement agents. Our problem at times is we get carried away and rush to do things on our own out of emotions and forget that we need to involve God first in everything. We can see the importance of this in many cases in the Bible where the presence of the servants of God in a situation ushers in a big breakthrough. For example, the presence of Prophet Elisha when the sons of the prophets went to the river Jordan to cut down logs and their axe head fell in the water and the son of a prophet cried to the servant of God for help because the axe was borrowed. Imagine if these sons of prophets had decided to go to the river Jordan to cut the logs on their own what would have happened to the borrowed axe and the owner. Our downfall at times is that we forget the servants of God and rush to do things on our own wanting to surprise them and we want to involve them when it's too late. Our endeavors fail because of this.

Another powerful example of how important it is to involve God in our situations is that of the wedding at Cana, when the wine ran out the host of the event had invited the Son of the living God who is Jesus Christ and when Mary the earthly mother of Jesus told Him that the wine was finished God was represented there, a miracle took place and water was turned into wine. I can hear someone saying was it alcoholic or non-alcoholic wine but let me tell you that does not matter for now I thank God that the master of ceremonies declared the wine as the best for last. There was a crisis of shortage of wine at a wedding at Cana and the problem was solved there and there.

Have you ever wondered why food stuff at weddings or parties is always limited, the answer is simple involve the presence of God through the Holy Spirit and everything will be enough with left overs? When you are about to start a journey pray to God before you even start the car and before you write an examination pray to God and the Holy Spirit will make you remember what you have been taught. If you are continually making mistakes at work and your bosses are always after you, change the way you do things by praying before you start your day, start your day with God and He will lead you to do your best throughout the day.

At one time, God took us to live in a foreign nation, from another foreign nation and we had left all our belongings. I remember we only carried a few items of clothing; we had no plates, cups, pots or even a spoon. When we arrived in that country we were planning to start from zero buying everything and we had no money to do so but we just believed in God, we had a lot of trust and faith in God that no matter what, we were sure that we would live happily in that nation. Just a day after we arrived we looked for a school for our children and eventually a place to stay near the school. A day after we moved into the new but empty apartment we were called down stairs by the security because there was a lorry which had come with goods. Upon hearing this we thought the driver of the lorry had come to the wrong apartment because we had never made any arrangements for anything to be delivered. We had given away all our belongings which we had left behind to men and women of God. I asked him if he was lost and he said he was not because he was told to come and call the pastor from Zimbabwe who had just arrived in the country, also the person who was giving us the items in the lorry was downstairs and yes it was for us! In great astonishment we went down stairs and found a widow and her son with a truck full of sofas, beds, pots, plates, spoons and a gas stove, in fact everything which is needed in a house was there. She told us that she had tried to sell those things for the past two years but could not find a buyer and so one night she dreamt, three times, that someone in white clothing told her that she should not sell the furniture because the owner is coming soon. She said she did not understand that dream until she saw us, that is when she felt that we are the servants of God to whom the household goods belonged. The moment she released the goods to us she said she felt peace inside. There were also many personal testimonies from this widow and her son from the time she gave us the goods. Her doors were opened because she gave to a servant of God who was in real need.

When God does a miracle it might sound like a fictitious movie but that is how He operates, we did not know this widow, but, for two years she had tried to sell her belongings and could not, she also told us that the more she looked for buyers the more vivid the dream of the person in white telling her not to sell the household goods became. When you faithfully serve the living God, surely you will speak of miracles every day of your life. Whatever situation you might be facing in your life today just remain focused in your faith in God and He will surely give you a miracle, no crisis is too difficult for Him He just desires to be involved in your life. If your marriage seems rocky today, do not worry just faithfully involve the presence of God everything will be well and okay.

This is how God operates at times of crisis, He does not come in his holy nature to physically perform miracles He comes in the form of other people especially those who have a willing heart to be used. In short God uses people to do miracles. At one-time God used David to kill Goliath but He had the power to strike Goliath down Himself since He was being mocked by this Philistine giant. Moses took the children of Israel from bondage in Egypt; do you think God was not capable of leading these Israelites alone to the Promised Land? Saul was used mightily by God from being a murderer to an apostle who preached in so many places. If you lack spiritual eyes you will miss the person or object bringing a miracle to you, thinking it's nothing special. Many assess people and try to evaluate them instead of receiving the message they are carrying from God. How many times have you looked down upon a certain servant of God just because of the way he or she was dressed, or how that servant of God spoke and thereby missed out on the real message being preached?

There are many people who have discovered their God given purpose in a time of a crisis. Not every crisis comes to bury or destroy you or your dreams but some come as a way of pushing you from your comfort zone to a place of receiving your God given purpose. For example, Saul the first king of Israel leaves home with a servant to look for his father's lost donkeys, but this crisis led him to Prophet

Samuel who ended up revealing the mystery of God in a crisis by telling him that he is the chosen first king of Israel. Imagine if there was no predicament of the missing donkeys Saul would not have had the chance to meet the Prophet Samuel. Also it would have been dangerous for Saul to be anointed in front of many people as it would have brought fighting in Israel.

David the son of Jesse was sent to deliver food and to check on his brothers who were at war with the Philistines and their giant who daily for 40 days ridiculed God, the children of Israel and their King Saul who was in hiding. David went to war carrying roasted maize and cheese as a mere shepherd boy but when he left the war zone he was a son in law of the King, his whole family had been exempted from paying tax. David was being praised by people singing that Saul had killed 10,000 but he had killed 100,000 this is what brewed the hatred between Saul and David, the moment David arrived God made sure he was in time to witness the giant Philistine's daily routine of mocking the children of Israel. When such an opportunity presented itself David grabbed it with both hands that is why he asked the baggage keeper what the reward was for anyone who would kill Goliath and against the discouragement of his brothers he remained focused. We all know the end of the story that predicament made David the next king of Israel. The main reason a lot of us miss the message and purpose of God in a crisis it is because of the attitude we have. We often rush to blame God or our surroundings and prematurely judge what we do not understand.

Let me bring to your attention to the situation in the home of Mary and Martha with their dead brother Lazarus. They could not understand why Jesus did not come on time to save the one He loved most, little did they know that the crisis was for the glory of God to be revealed and we all know the end result the dead and smelly Lazarus came back to life straight from the tomb. If Jesus Christ was present when Lazarus died like what Mary and Martha wanted, then the glory of God would not have manifested for the people to witness. Jesus knew about Lazarus' death He even told His disciples about this. But he delayed for those days because He knew that if He rushed there the miracle would not have been of much significance since according to the custom of where Lazarus lived a person could come back to life after a day of being dead, so after three days of being dead the miracle became noteworthy.

Pay attention to God in every crisis knowing that everything works for good to those who love the Lord especially those called according to His purpose. Do not blame or be angry with God during a crisis because it might have come to present the greatness and mystery of God in a crisis. Not all predicaments bring death some come as a teaching, some come as proof to those who believe that there is no God. Who knows you might be the next testimony for many people to believe that we are all what we are in this world because there is God in heaven who had created us all.

Chapter six: Corona crisis

The year 2020 has not been a very good year it has affected the whole world, everything was brought to a standstill because of the corona virus also known as covid19 crisis. We all know that this virus is said to have originated in China and then spread quickly to the whole world like a veld fire on a summer afternoon. People were dying in their thousands every day in hospitals and old peoples' homes around the world and also many were being infected every day. The world became very scary and dangerous to live in and we at one point thought that maybe the world is coming to an end as foretold in the word of God. Travelling became restricted and even if one wanted to travel, the situation was so scary and dangerous that very few were brave enough to travel in a world where everyone was told to stay indoors for safety. No one was moving around everyone was so afraid that staying indoors was the best solution. Towns and cities became like ghost towns, there was no movement especially that of the general public. Nurses, doctors, police, soldiers and in some cases ambulances were the regulars moving about. People were ordered to wear masks whenever they left their houses and in many nations it became mandatory to wear masks in public, in some cases a fine was imposed but like I said who would ignore what's safe in order to live. Bars, gyms, restaurants, hotels, schools, non-grocery shops, theatres, stadiums, churches were all completely closed, and even if they were open who would dare risk their life in such a daunting situation. At one time it was even scary and stressful to watch news because it was all about new cases and new deaths being reported every hour.

Since it was a major crisis for the whole world no nation was spared from this pandemic, but even though the situation was immense and confusing does not mean that God was no longer active, He was and He is still God because He does not change forever. In such a crisis like the corona pandemic I know there are many who are still mourning their beloved ones whom they lost but also there are others who were so sick and were put on a ventilator and still survived, some died before going to the hospital and some survived without seeking any medical attention which was miraculous. Others were put on the very same ventilators and yet did not make it. I also know that there are many people who have testimonies because of the same pandemic which made others mourn.

I know some businesses that opened because of the corona virus, for example I know someone who started a food delivery business during this period. He looked at what was needed most and noticed that everyone was afraid of death but people still needed to eat. Food is an essential part of our lives and without it we die. Sometimes God can give you a big testimony during a crisis period. Did anyone ever imagine that at one point we will all be wearing masks as we go about our daily lives and did anyone think that masks would be a big business in this world? We were all accustomed to seeing masks worn by medical staff in clinics, hospitals etc. On the same note someone today is smiling all the way to the bank because of the industry of manufacturing masks during this corona pandemic. God opened some people's eyes to see a need and to rapidly act and supply what was essential to everyone. Home-made masks became a hit because these were made with fabric and were easy to wash re use, not like the ones used by medical staff.

All of a sudden social media grabbed all the attention as everyone wanted to hear what was happening worldwide. At one point most people were seeing social media as a tool for entertainment and amusement but those same platforms began to be used responsibly and business wise as many people became entrepreneurs. As the crisis deepened most people by the grace of God began to see many business opportunities which allowed them to make fortunes out of this. Everyone began to appreciate the power of social media because information was readily available. Many businesses marketed their products on social media and it caused them to go global because of such a serious pandemic.

Whenever there is a crisis God does not make you look useless, being God He knows what's good for us and He always makes sure He provides whatever is necessary for each one of us as long we have laid it down before Him. You and I have seen this day because of the greatness of

God who fought for all of us in times of battles such as sickness, accidents, viruses, or any other crisis or pandemic like cyclones or tsunamis which we have encountered in life. Being alive today and not crediting that to God Almighty is a sin, we all need to know and appreciate that it is this same God who gives us life and who also has power to end our life. Whenever there is a crisis in our lives we all need to look to God for deliverance and it will surely come. Never make the mistake of running to the wrong source when encountering problems in life. All world leaders should look to God for solutions to the challenges we are all facing. Without God the world will or can be nothing. All the medical practitioners who were being called front liners during the corona pandemic were protected and covered by the hand of God. They too need God so that they are able to execute their tasks with diligence and without fear.

When a crisis occurs, even if it brings sorrows and death, it does not stop the greatness of God from being seen. I still believe if it was not because of the greatness of this

God many people including you and I were supposed to have died because of this corona virus. God has once again saved us all, it could have been worse had it not been for Him. The same way God has fought for you when you were supposed to die in a crisis of malaria, earthquake or road accident is the same way he has done it during corona crisis and He will keep doing it when any other pandemic and crises may arise in the future as long you believe in Him. As children of God or as human beings we need to be thankful that our heavenly Father who is the creator of the heavens and earth is always there for us and He can always fight and win any battle for us.

Even if the world economy is going down because of the corona effects I believe as long we all keep trusting in God He will surely see us through this crisis, when we know who to cry to we do not have to worry. I am sure God will give all those people who were affected by the corona crisis a miracle and comfort that they will forget it quickly, I pray for healing to those who are sick and for those who have lost their loved ones because of corona virus. Testimonies don't just happen; they originate and are manufactured by God Himself. Whatever you are suffering from today or whatever you call a crisis today as long you and I believe in God we will have a testimony or a big miracle on the way. You might be crying about a missed opportunity during this crisis, maybe you were supposed to be married during this time and everything was postponed because gatherings were being restricted do not worry, God might have allowed that to happen to protect you from the unthinkable, remember destiny delayed is not destiny denied.

I know of a God fearing sister who was supposed to be married in May of this year 2020 of corona pandemic and since the lockdown started in March the guy could not raise enough money because business was slow. Eventually as time went on he kept postponing the lobola or bride price until the relationship broke up, the young lady cried uncontrollably because she was hoping she would be married to this guy, but to the greatness of God within few months of break up the woman was proposed by another gentleman who was ready to marry her with all resources at his disposal. I am not saying this young lady was a loose person but I am sure it was God who had seen her crying and brought her someone to answer her cries, remember the theme of the book, the mysteries of God in a crisis. Who knows maybe the first guy was not meant for her and this corona crisis came to fight for her, this is just my thinking. Who knows she might have cried feeling disappointed when it might have been actually God working mysteriously during a crisis of her life to give her a real husband. Whenever you see a way out of a crisis in life never ever think it is your wise ways at work but instead you need to see God in that. Sometimes God removes us from our will and directs or positions us in line with His will. Ask yourself how many times you have felt that what you are crying for is worth so much to you and then God diverts you to something greater which you have never thought of.

A former church member told me how he got a breakthrough to buy his first car and a residential stand during this corona crisis period. I asked him how he managed to do it in such a period and he said if it was not God who gave him the scones and cakes making business idea during lockdown he could have never thought of such in any way in his life, He told me that he watched how to make cakes and scones on YouTube because he had never been a baker in his life and the idea was to make one for his family and from there he started to receive orders from people in his community until the business grew from making 100 scones a day to making 500 and above per day. That is how God answers prayers in a crisis, he was getting stressed about how he was supposed to feed his family in a time of crisis and he got a clean business idea that ended up giving him more than what he was earning at his work. God made him a businessman from being employed under someone; he was telling me that he is now looking at a bigger scale in order to meet the demand from his customers. So whenever a crisis comes in life we need our spiritual eyes to open and show us the right way to take, some of us did not see any business ideas coming in a crisis because of how we relate to God. Even if you try your best, as long as you do not have a good relationship with God you might not see anything. Remember God comes in when there is a crisis somewhere somehow. This gentleman started this to solve a crisis of bread in his family and it grew to be a big business and as I am writing this book he is all over the news with this business. How many times have you said I cannot do this and that because I am not qualified to do it or this is not my line of business?

Another testimony I got from a friend mine is of how he managed to drill a borehole at his home during the months of corona lockdown in Zimbabwe. I asked him where he got the money from when it was known that he was not getting any pay during corona crisis lockdown. He told me that he was fed up of waking up and eating, drinking and sleeping and so he thought of starting a vegetable gardening project at his house as a way of exercising and whiling up time. He grew many types of vegetables and within three months the whole community and shops were coming to buy from him and that lead him to earn a lot of money within a short space of time. I told him that this it is a big testimony and it is only God who gives such ideas in a crisis like this, hallelujah.

A similar testimony is of a widow whom I know who survived throughout the corona crisis, getting food everyday but she was not working, she told me that she did not even remember some of the people who were giving her food; Don't you think she was being fed by angels and her children during this crisis period? She even jokingly remarked that she began to share with others what she was getting. I read in newspapers and other sources of many people who started businesses when there was a crisis and most of such businesses stay forever. What is born in a crisis usually stays long and grows bigger because most people value what comes during times of tears. This crisis brought up new forms of doing businesses and the way people conduct business meetings even changed. The UN meetings were done online with all heads of states in their homes and offices. This gave network and internet service providers a lot of businesses in a crisis.

Corona crisis might be something that most people in the world cried about but I am of the opinion that still in that crisis many saw the greatness of God in some different ways. There are a lot of cases which we have experienced the greatness of God in one way or the other. Being alive is the biggest testimony especially when one thinks of how many people died who were even more cautious than yourself in all the precautions. Same applies in some of the stories I have quoted from the Bible in other chapters where we have seen the hand of God, but during that same time there were other people who were left crying. That is how God works His ways are not the ways of man, or His mind is not like the mind of man. He is God and He does not need to consult with anyone when He wants to do things.

Chapter seven.

How to Experience an Atmosphere of Signs, Wonders and Miracles?

Do you want to see the supernatural in your life? Here is how you can experience signs, wonders and miracles where you need them most.

The supernatural. People all over the world desire to experience the miraculous—to see and experience those things that are over and above the norm, beyond, higher, surpassing and outside the natural realm. But for most, particularly nonbelievers, life is limited to the earthly realm, conforming to the ordinary course of nature and those things that can be deduced by human reasoning alone.

As born-again believers, that is not where we are meant to reside! We are created to walk and live in the supernatural and to experience supernatural healing, provision, favor, deliverance and protection. We are living in a time right now when we need to know how to live in the supernatural—to experience signs, wonders and miracles. "Rejoice! And renew your faith in the supernatural!"

If you need a miracle in your life—your victory is waiting for you in the supernatural. Here is how you can experience signs, wonders and miracles where you need them most.

1. Believe the love of God

"We have come to know and have believed the love which God has for us." –1 John 4:16 (NASB)

Do you need a miracle? Love is the answer. You may be thinking money is the answer, healing is the answer, or deliverance is the answer. But those are just the manifestations of the real power behind every miracle— the love of God.

You see, you will never walk in the realm of the miraculous until you understand the love God has for you and for all people. We're not just talking about any love, but **THE LOVE**. Because **GOD IS LOVE**. He doesn't have love. **HE IS LOVE!**

First John 4:16 says, *"And we have known and believed the love that God has for us. God is love, and he who abides in love abides in God, and God in him" (NKJV).* Notice in this verse it says, "We have known and believed the love." To believe is to have faith in His love. Most Christians don't have faith in His love. If you were to ask them if God loves them, most would say yes, but they don't really believe it. They just mentally agree with John 3:16. *'For God so loved the world that he gave his one and only Son, that whoever believes in him shall not perish but have eternal life'.*

Consider Mark 4:37-38: *"And a great windstorm arose, and the waves beat into the boat, so that it was already filling. But He was in the stern, asleep on a pillow. And they awoke Him and said to Him, "Teacher, do You not care that we are perishing?" (NKJV).* Love Himself was asleep in that boat—the same One who was moved with compassion and healed their sick. Compassion is not a feeling; it's a Person. Jesus said, *"The Father who dwells in me does the work" (John 14:10, NKJV).* It's the Father, who is LOVE, who does the work. People today often think and say the same thing Jesus' disciples said in that boat: "How come You let this come on me, Lord? Don't You care?" What is that? It's unbelief! In what? **THE LOVE—WHO IS GOD—WHO IS LOVE.**

To have faith in God is to have faith in love itself. Faith works by love. Without believing in the love of God for YOU, you will not be able to fuel the kind of faith it takes to experience signs, wonders and miracles in your life. To develop your faith in God's love, or in anything else from God, you have to learn what the Word says about it. *"Faith comes by hearing, and hearing by the word of God" (Romans 10:17, NKJV).*

For instance, Psalm 23:6, NKJV, says, *"Surely goodness and mercy shall follow me all the days of my life."* Put that verse from the Word in first place. Don't ever go by how you feel about the love of God. Don't confess anything else. Be confident in the fact that God's mercy and goodness will follow you all the days of your life. If you have the idea today that God is not willing to partner in your deal with you-you aren't believing the love of God.

Maybe you're saying, "Well, I just don't know what to do."

Well, it's praising time when you don't know what to do. Start by praising. Then, fill up on the Word! Ask yourself this: Are you spending enough time with God? What are you spending the most time on? The television or Him? You're going to have to ask yourself that question, because if you're not spending any time with Him, sickness is coming; trouble is coming.

Start by reading 1 John every day for two weeks. Meditate on the scriptures concerning God's love—it will develop your capacity for faith. As your faith grows, your understanding of God's love will expand until Satan's tactics begin to shrink and lose their grip over your life. Then, you'll become a prime candidate for experiencing signs, wonders and miracles.

Settle this forever—healing belongs to you, deliverance belongs to you, victory is your inheritance. However, the ball is in your court. You don't have to try to get God to manifest a miracle in your life. Love already provided everything for you. But it starts with believing. Say this: *"I believe the love is in me now. I believe it never fails. I believe God is Love."*

2. Receive the Love of God

"And I pray that you, being rooted and established in love, may have power, together with all the Lord's holy people, to grasp how wide and long and high and deep is the love of Christ, and to know this love that surpasses knowledge—that you may be filled to the measure of all the fullness of God." –Ephesians 3:17-19 (NIV)

Believing is the foundation, but so many people stop short of receiving the love of God. They don't feel worthy, they fear He won't come through for them, or they fear He is able but maybe not willing—at least not for them. They camp out on past failures and they put themselves in the position of judge and jury—rather than God who declared them innocent with the blood of Jesus.

Unworthiness, guilt and shame all stem from fear, and the enemy is lingering, waiting to use your fear as a back door to steal the inventory outlined in the Word of God that belongs to you. That's why healing, prosperity and deliverance always come, but they aren't always received. But there's one way to keep what God has given to you—and it's to receive the love of God without fear.

Fear is a thief. Fear will block the miraculous in your life. In the Gospel of Luke, we get an up-close view of how Jesus dealt with fear when a man was facing a serious trial:

Then a man named Jairus, a synagogue leader, came and fell at Jesus' feet, pleading with him to come to his house because his only daughter, a girl of about twelve, was dying…. While Jesus was still speaking, someone came from the house of Jairus, the synagogue leader. "Your daughter is dead," he said. "Don't bother the teacher anymore." Hearing this, Jesus said to Jairus, *"Don't be afraid; just believe, and she will be healed" (Luke 8:41-42, 49-50, NIV).*

Why was Jesus so quick to tell Jairus not to fear? Because He knew fear would hinder Jairus from receiving. Fear tolerated is faith contaminated—that's a spiritual fact. Fear will prevent your miracle from taking place. And if you couldn't do something about fear, Jesus wouldn't have told Jairus to stop it. What gets rid of fear? Love-filled faith will cast it out. Focusing on receiving the love of God will stop fear in its tracks. Believing and receiving the love of God will put your focus in the right place to experience signs, wonders and miracles.

If you're believing for healing today, one thing is true— God has done all He's going to do about healing you. Maybe you're thinking, Well, then how come I'm not healed if I'm healed? Because you keep saying you're not, and you have what you say. If you want to experience signs, wonders and miracles, you have to receive the love of God with your words. Change your words, change your outcome.

Make it official today—receive the love of God—gather the scriptures you're standing on to receive the miracle you need. If it is healing, for example, gather those scriptures, and speak them over your situation by faith. Then, rejoice as you receive!

When you get to that point, where you're rejoicing before you receive, there's no going back. It doesn't matter what pain or what demon comes against you. You have received love and faith will boil over. You just stay in the Word, and it'll boil because faith is coming. Faith is coming. You can't feel it, but it's coming. You keep the water on the heat, and it will boil. Amen. That's believing in and receiving the love of God.

3. Release the Love of God

"Love never fails." –1 Corinthians 13:5 (NKJV) If you aren't experiencing signs, wonders and miracles—it's time to check your love walk to be sure you are releasing the love of God that you have believed and received. When you walk in love, you release a force to work on your behalf—a force that has all the appearance of weakness, but is stronger than any force in existence.

A critical part of experiencing signs, wonders and miracles is acting on the Word concerning the love of God. To walk in love is to step aside and allow the power of the love of God to come between you and the situation with which you are dealing. First John 4:11-12 says, *"Beloved, if God so loved us, we also ought to love one another. No one has seen God at any time. If we love one another, God abides in us, and His love has been perfected in us" (NKJV).* The Word perfected means "allowed to run its full course." By practicing this love on one another, the love of God is perfected, or allowed to run its full course, in us. By acting on the Word of God and allowing the love of God, which is perfect, to run its full course in our lives, we keep the gates open for signs, miracles and wonders.

There are two ways to perfect the love of God in your life: By keeping the Word of God in your eyes, heart and mouth, and by practicing love on others. Love takes practice, and we can practice on each other. You won't operate perfectly in love at the very beginning; but as you persist, you will get increasingly better at it. If you fail, simply confess it as sin, receive your forgiveness and go on. Keep loving. Keep overlooking the shortcomings of other people. Look for Jesus in them. Forgive immediately and stay out of offense. Decide to live the love life. Make the quality decision to live by love, and you'll keep the door open to the miracle you need.

In conclusion, believing, receiving and releasing the love of God is the ticket to signs, wonders and miracles—there's no way around it. No amount of prayer, serving, pleading or Scripture memorization can take its place. Love has always been the answer. If you've been believing for healing, financial breakthrough or deliverance for a long time, put your focus on love. It NEVER fails.

TRUTH AFFIRMATIONS

I AFFIRM that:

I am like a tree planted by the rivers of water, my leaves are evergreen and shall never wither.

I am flourishing like the cedars of Lebanon.

I am not subject to dryness when it comes.

I function under the unction of the Holy Spirit and I know all things.

I am like the city set on a hill,

I cannot be hidden.

I am the light of the world.

I am the salt of the earth,

I preserve the earth.

I do not walk in darkness because my path is that of a shining light that shines brighter and brighter unto the perfect day.

I am walking in divine health because I have the life of God in me, from the crown of my head to the soles of my feet. Every fiber of my being, every bone of my body, every cell of my blood is inundated with the life of God.

I am a champion for life.

Prosperity is mine,

Favor is mine.

My victory is sure.

I am making progress,

I am moving forward and upward only, there is no stagnation in my life.

I am a success for life because of the Holy Spirit. I deal excellently in all my affairs, none of my feet shall ever slide. I have an excellent spirit.

The wisdom of God is at work in me mightily, I know what to do, what to say, who to meet at the right time.

I never miss my way.

The knowledge of God is increasing in my life.

God's grace multiples upon my life.

I increase in Grace which produces in my life, beauty, honor, acceptability, loveliness, goodwill, benefits, endurance, promotion, elegance, charm, glory....

I increase in divine favor.

I increase in speed and accuracy.

No weapon formed against me shall ever prosper. Greater is He who is in me than he that is in the world.

The lines are falling unto me in pleasant places, yes I have a Godly heritage. Ministering Angels are at my disposal, working for me.

I am a world overcomer.

I am more than a conqueror.

All things are orchestrated for my benefit.

I cannot be disadvantaged in any way, it's all working together for my good because I love the Lord.

My finances are booming all the time, I lay up gold as dust.

I increase in fortune.

Great is my peace and prosperity.

I am a great personality, I have access to all nations, no limitations, no boundaries.

The glory of God is risen upon me; I am the effulgence of God's divine presence. God tabernacles in me, I carry His atmosphere of miracles everywhere I go.

I am strengthened,

Energized,

Endued with power,

Ability and might.

I am a great minister of the Gospel of our Lord Jesus Christ.

I am an ardent soul winner.

The Word of God prospers in my life and fulfills in me what it talks about.

I can do all things through Christ who strengthens me.

I am who God says I am.

I am a blessing to my world and everything

I lay my hands upon prospers and is blessed. Kings are coming to my rising. My future is bright and glorious, I cannot fail, and neither can I be defeated.

I win always, in every situation.

Every mountain before me is made plain, all crooked paths are made straight.

I am the head and not the tail.

Any careless word that I have spoken or has been spoken concerning me is nullified in Jesus' name.

Grace and peace are multiplied unto me.

Springs of joy wells up within me all the time. The Word of God is effective in my life.

I am super-favored,

I live in super-abundance because

I am connected to God's unending supply system.

The love of God is shed abroad in my heart and this love radiates to all around me.

Nothing can stop me, nothing can hinder me.

The hand of God rests upon me and my household. I function from the position of rest, I live a struggle free, worry free life all the time... Oh glory to God!!!!!!

I thank You for qualifying me to be a partaker of the inheritance of the saints in light. Darkness has no place in me, for I am native-born to the light.

I manifest this light to my world ever so brightly today and always I walk in the light, as He is in the light.

I walk in glory, Strength, Victory, Success,

Prosperity and righteousness today. My life is the manifestation of the wisdom and grace of God!

I am what God says I am.

I testify to the faithfulness of God. I testify to the grace of God in my life. And I testify to the efficacy of the Word of God in me and through me.

I declare that I am fruitful and productive always, in the mighty Name of Jesus Christ!

Closing Prayer.

Dear Lord I thank you for always fighting for me when I face battles, thank you for all the unconditional love you always give everyone in this world. Thank you God Almighty for protecting me and my family in times of battles and crisis and thank you for giving us victories throughout the way. I pray that you would help everyone who might be facing different challenges, storms and battles right now in Jesus' Name, heal those who are sick in the name of your only Son Jesus Christ, wipe every tear flowing off the cheeks of those who are crying right now because of different reasons. Many people are facing many challenges and crisis out there and it is my prayer right now that you show your greatness to those who are in crisis right now, I also pray for peace in the whole world and that wars and fighting amongst humankind would stop. I pray for recovering of all businesses which suffered during corona crisis and any other business which are not doing well right now, Oh Lord I pray for marriages which are waiting for a miracle from you right now that they can be sweet. I pray for those who cannot afford decent food and clothing that you may raise ravens in their lives which can provide for them in Jesus' Name. Finally let those who have no chance and choice to receive Jesus Christ as their saviour do so now so that they can also enjoy the miracles you can offer in life. I pray in faith that you may hear this prayer today in Jesus' Name, Amen.

If anyone have never accepted Lord Jesus Christ as a personal Savior then should pray from the heart following the prayer below. ***Romans 10: 9-10: 9 If you declare with your mouth, "Jesus is Lord," and believe in your heart that God raised him from the dead, you will be saved. 10 For it is with your heart that you believe and are justified, and it is with your mouth that you profess your faith and are saved.***

Dear Lord Jesus, I know that I am a sinner, and I ask for Your forgiveness. I believe You died for my sins and rose from the dead. I turn from my sins and invite You to come into my heart and life. I want to trust and follow You as my Lord and Savior.

HALLELUJAH!

GLORY TO GOD, TO GOD FOREVER AND EVER! AMEN!!

For Further Counseling and Prayers

jchinamo@gmail.com